THE NEW AMERICAN STEAKHOUSE COOKBOOK

THE NEW
AMERICAN

STEAKHOUSE
COOKBOOK

It's Not Just Meat and Potatoes Anymore

DAVID WALZOG and
ANDREW FRIEDMAN

Broadway Books
New York

BROADWAY

PRINTED IN THE UNITED STATES OF AMERICA

BROADWAY BOOKS and its logo, a letter B bisected on the diagonal, are trademarks of Random House, Inc.

Visit our Web site at www.broadwaybooks.com

First edition published 2005

Book design by Platinum Design Inc., NYC
Photography by Shimon and Tammar Rothstein
Photo of French fries on page 144 courtesy Getty Images/Digital Vision. Photo of martini glasses on page 22 courtesy Image Source/Alamy. Photo of sauce dishes on page 170 courtesy ImageState Royalty Free/Alamy

Library of Congress
Cataloging-in-Publication Data
Walzog, David.
    The new American steakhouse cookbook : its not just meat and potatoes anymore / by David Walzog and Andrew Friedman.— 1st ed.
        p. cm.
    Includes index.
    1. Cookery, American. I. Friedman, Andrew, 1967– II. Title.

TX715.W2375 2005
641.5973—dc22
2004057050

ISBN 0-7679-1943-2

10 9 8 7 6 5 4 3 2 1

I dedicate this book to the guests of Strip House, Michael Jordan's The Steak House NYC, and The Steak House at the Monkey Bar. Creating a dining experience for you on a daily and nightly basis is my greatest source of professional pride. You inspired this book and, in many ways, made it possible. Thank you.

ACKNOWLEDGMENTS

Over the past year, I've learned that writing a book is a lot like running a kitchen: a team of people working together toward a common goal. My sincere thanks to the following:

My co-author, Andrew Friedman, for his help in guiding me through my first book, taking what I told him (occasionally in kitchen-speak) and transforming it into the text of this book. He's a true pro and a fantastic friend;

My agent, Angela Miller, for her help honing the New American steakhouse message;

My editor, Jennifer Josephy, for her guidance, support, and thoughtful notes along the way;

Stephen Rubin, president and publisher of Doubleday, for his interest in and enthusiasm for this project from its earliest stages;

Sharon Bowers, a super-professional recipe tester, who worked at a breakneck pace with a smile on her face, and helped ensure that the words in this book add up to great flavors in your home;

Shimon and Tammar Rothstein, two excellent photographers who took one delicious photo after another;

Allyson Giard, Jennifer Josephy's assistant, for her consistently pleasant presence and help along the way;

Jono Moratis, for providing the beer and wine lists at the back of the book. When you see how often you refer to them, you'll want to thank him yourself;

Rene Lenger, Strip House's chef de cuisine, for his hard work and dedication;

All of the staff at all of the restaurants. You guys make it look easy and give me the confidence to keep pushing ahead;

Penny, Peter, and Mathew Glazier, my restaurant partners, for setting the stage with the restaurants where we've honed our brand of New American steakhouse cooking. Their friendship, trust, and collaboration inspire me to keep up our standards and never stop evolving;

My parents, for not saying "no" when I told them I wanted to become a chef;

My wife, Miki, for always allowing me to follow my dreams, and for her tolerance of the long, grueling schedules that the restaurants demand;

My stepson, Shay, for being an enthusiastic presence at any and all steak dinners;

My daughters, Mikayla and Georgia, for their young palates and willingness to try anything that Daddy cooks.

CONTENTS

INTRODUCTION

I bet you think of the same things I do when you imagine the perfect steakhouse experience.

It begins out in the parking lot with the smoky, char-tinged aroma that wafts out of the kitchen vents and ropes you in. It continues at the bar, with a bracingly cold vodka martini, a flotilla of paper-thin ice rafts on its surface, and a pile of jumbo olives resting in its depths. And it culminates, often for several hours, at the table. I pace myself, beginning the feast with something relatively light to perk up my appetite, such as shrimp cocktail—the sauce alive with horseradish, lemon juice, and garlic—and a salad, either tomato and onion, or a chopped vegetable salad with smoked bacon and red wine vinaigrette.

Then comes the main event, the thing I've been fantasizing about and fasting for all day, a huge slab of perfectly charred steak, the crust formed by cracked black pepper, dry-aged beef, and salt, all fused together by the flame of the grill. On the side, creamed spinach and crisped potatoes, plus a generous pour of red Burgundy or California Cabernet filling a big, round wineglass.

The evening's indulgence wraps up with the drama of the Dessert Decision: the waiter's offering, the table's feigned hesitation ("We really shouldn't . . ."), and the acquiescence ("Oh, all right"). This is no time for sorbet or a fruit plate. Instead the table fills with chocolate cake, cheesecake, and hot fudge sundaes. Finally, there's coffee or perhaps an after-dinner drink, rituals that extend the evening a bit longer, giving everyone a chance to reflect on the meal before going their separate ways, or heading home for a long, deep night's sleep.

After a buildup like that, you might think that when it comes to steakhouses, my motto would be "If it ain't broke, don't fix it."

I wish that were the case. But as much as I've always loved the idea and ideal of steakhouses, I have to admit that in reality I always found them vaguely disappointing. When I became a professional chef, I was finally able to put my finger on what was lacking. In fact, there were things that started to bother me about steakhouses, like the drab surroundings, the gruff waiters, and the utter predictability of the menu. I think a great meal, like a great movie, always has at least one good twist, and there are simply no surprises in the traditional steakhouse meal.

It never occurred to me that one day I'd have a chance to do something about this, much less become one of the best-known practitioners of steakhouse cooking in New York City. Then, in 1998, my restaurant partners, Penny and Peter Glazier, and I decided to attempt one of the most unthinkable tasks one could embark on in the New York restaurant world: to reinvigorate the steakhouse by creating a new take on the genre, bucking a tradition that dates back to before I was born. In other words, to go head-to-head with the entrenched steakhouse establishments, offering a modernized version more in sync with the contemporary palate and expectations of today's gastronomically evolved Americans.

One of the reasons I never expected to find myself behind the stoves of a steakhouse is that I'm a member of a generation of chefs who cook New American cuisine, bringing a whole slew of influences and creativity to the plate. I trained at modern institutions such as Gotham Bar and Grill, then became known for southwestern food at Arizona 206 and Tapika. To my peers and me steakhouses were old school, right up there with stuffy French joints and hotel restaurants on the list of places we wouldn't have been caught dead cooking.

But here I am today, proudly cooking at three of New York's most popular steakhouses, Michael Jordan's The Steak House NYC in Grand Central Terminal, Strip House in downtown Manhattan, and The Steak House at the Monkey Bar in Midtown, as well as Strip Houses in Livingston, New Jersey, and Houston, Texas. And now, looking back with 20-20 hindsight, it makes perfect sense: one of the defining traits of my generation of American chefs is our reverence for fresh, seasonal ingredients and bringing out their natural beauty and flavor. In that context, selecting, seasoning, and cooking what is perceived by many as a simple piece of protein is as pure a challenge as any chef could ask for.

There's another reason that my evolving into a steakhouse specialist seems natural in retrospect: Americans can't claim credit for many culinary conventions; the French and Italians cornered those markets before our country was even founded. But the steakhouse is a distinctly American invention, so why shouldn't an American chef like me see what he could do with the conventions of the category?

I don't necessarily call what I do at our restaurants New American cuisine. Instead, I call it New American steakhouse cooking, because I've put my own spin on steakhouse classics, just as I used to update southwestern dishes, and as my contemporaries have overhauled everything from Italian to Indian food. And I've pulled it off in the most competitive testing ground in the world, New York City. It's steakhouse cooking that bears my own personal stamp, or maybe I should say my brand.

At all of my restaurants, I see firsthand what a steakhouse experience means to people. Just as it was for my family when I was a kid, a steakhouse meal is a special treat, an indulgence of the diet and the wallet. So what we do at the restaurants carries an enormous responsibility: we strive to deliver nothing less than the best steakhouse meal of our customers' lives. I hope that doesn't sound arrogant. I sure don't mean it as a boast; it's just a measure of how much we respect our customers and appreciate their business.

This book will teach you everything I know about buying, preparing, and cooking meat (as well as fish and poultry), and share more than 100 recipes for my updated and original steakhouse cocktails, starters, side dishes, and desserts. In other words, everything you need to make a modern steakhouse dinner at home.

EVOLUTION OF A NEW AMERICAN STEAKHOUSE

One day in 1997, I found myself walking along the balcony overlooking the Vanderbilt Avenue side of Grand Central Terminal, kicking around restaurant concepts with Peter and Penny Glazier, a restaurateur couple with whom I had worked on a previous project.

Like many who moved to New York in the 1980s, when quality of life here was dwindling, I considered Grand Central past its prime, to put it mildly. But it was in the midst of a renaissance: the cathedral-high ceilings were being restored and the place was beginning to show signs of its long-lost grandeur. The balcony was in the early stages of a demolition followed by a renovation, so it took quite a bit of imagination to envision its potential.

Peter and Penny had secured this gem of a location and despite the tarps and scaffolding that obscured the view, it was clear that they had made an excellent call: with more than half a million passersby every day (roughly the population of Cincinnati), Grand Central was one of the most heavily trafficked buildings in the country, even when it was deteriorating by the month. Just imagine how popular it might be after it was polished back to mint condition.

We discussed a number of ideas that day. Peter made a suggestion that would set the next several years of our professional lives in motion: "What about a steakhouse?" His astute observation was that a steakhouse would be the perfect establishment for this marbled sanctuary through which commuters and tourists passed on their way in and out of the city. As you may know, there's a place called the Oyster Bar that's been thriving on Grand Central's lower level for decades, so why not a steakhouse on the upper level?

Just a few days later, lightning struck: we learned that basketball superstar Michael Jordan was hunting for a space for a steakhouse he wanted to open in New York City. And just like that, we were developing Michael Jordan's The Steak House NYC. With our landmark location and a living sports legend on board, it seemed like a slam dunk.

Everyone expects great beef at a steakhouse, but I wanted to have great everything. I milked my network of purveyors for all it was worth, bringing in the same superior fruits and vegetables I had become accustomed to using in other restaurants. I also brought my plating techniques to the show. We served a pretty traditional menu but took lots of pride in the side dishes and other offerings. Even an appetizer like a tomato and onion salad looked and tasted like never before, magnificently composed and full of fresh-from-the-farm flavor. In the *New York Times,* Ruth Reichl said that we "reworked the standard steakhouse menu with energy and imagination" and called the rib eye steak "a tribute to the American steer."

I first began to cook and serve what I think of as New American steakhouse cooking a few years later when we launched Strip House on 12th Street in 2000. This restaurant is a sly throwback to old-time steakhouses of a different sort. Strip House is dimly lit and done up in bordello red. It's a nod to the kind of place where you might have spotted the Rat Pack when they dropped in on New York City together. Contributing to this effect is the Glaziers' knack for selecting landmark locations that recall a fabled era of restaurant-going, such as marrying the Hotel Elysée's restaurant to its famous Monkey Bar in Midtown and turning the old Asti Italian restaurant space on 12th Street into Strip House, making it look as if it had been there for generations.

At Strip House, with its downtown location and slightly more interpretive decor, I took a more dramatic stab at modernizing the steakhouse. One of the secrets of our success has been that we rethink rather than discard classic offerings, so the food feels familiar and fresh at the same time: our creamed spinach is infused with truffle oil, the cocktail sauce is homemade, and we bring a seasonal approach to steakhouse cooking, varying the salads, soups, sides, and specials to reflect the time of year.

Some off-the-bat hits were Crisp Goose Fat Potatoes (which you can make at home with extra virgin olive oil in place of goose fat), Garlic-Parmesan Potato Chips, Batter-Fried Onions, Michael's Macaroni and Cheese, and Gruyère Potato Gratin.

THE QUESTION

There are recipes in this book for all of those side dishes, not to mention fish, poultry, and meats that go beyond beef, all cooked with a steakhouse sensibility, by which I mean big portions and big flavors. But I first got the idea to write a cookbook because of one question that my customers ask me over and over:

"How do you do it?"

It's a question that refers to the beef and how we cook it. They want to know why the meat tastes so good and stays so juicy, how we get the same perfect char on each and every steak, and the secrets to getting their requested doneness just right.

It's no exaggeration to say that I can't walk through the dining room of one of our restaurants without at least a few customers stopping me and asking "the question." I understand where they're coming from. When people buy and cook steak, they spend almost as much money as they do dining out, not to mention the price of their time.

In the pages that follow, you'll learn all of my secrets. The truth is that they're actually pretty simple. For example, most of our customers think there's some magic dust we sprinkle on the steaks to get that elusive char. But we actually use only salt and pepper, a hot grill (you can substitute a cast-iron pan if you need to), and a keen eye.

The other reason I wanted to write this book was to share my own personal home-cooking experience.

I find myself cooking entire meals from the restaurants at home. Whether it's steak or an alternative like a roasted half chicken or piece of swordfish, the golden roasted or grilled look of these main courses, the size of the portion, and the simplicity of presentation are both easy and impressive. And the side dishes have universal appeal, not to mention the fact that most of them go with any fish or meat you're serving.

RECURRING THEMES

In this book you'll notice that I employ a number of recurring ingredients, techniques, and preferences that you should keep in mind for your own cooking, whether or not it has anything to do with steaks and steakhouses.

FLAVOR BURSTS. I love food that surprises you from bite to bite. To make this happen, I often scatter ingredients in a deliberately haphazard way throughout a dish. For example, my vegetable rolls offer a different herb or combination of herbs in each mouthful, and my bruschetta-style tomatoes have bits of cracked black pepper lying in wait to spring unexpected flashes of heat on your palate.

THE POWER OF LEMON. I use lemon juice, grated lemon zest, and Lemon Vinaigrette (page 11) a lot in my cooking. The pleasing acidity of lemon acts as a sensory spotlight, perking up and highlighting other flavors. From salad dressings to soups to sauces, there are endless ways to use lemon in day-to-day cooking, especially in vegetable dishes and heavy, egg-based sauces and salad dressings.

INTERACTIVE FOOD. In most of the restaurants where I've been the chef, including all of the steakhouses I run today, diners are invited to mix and match various components of the meal, whether by sharing a table full of appetizers or customizing their main courses with side dishes and sauces. This is just as much fun at home as it is in a restaurant, and it's also a lot easier on the home cook because you don't have to time everything to be ready at exactly the same moment, or worry about plating them together. You just set out the components and let everyone compose their own dish.

FLAVOR CROWDS. Maybe it's because I'm a New Yorker that I don't seem to mind having a lot going on in a small space. In fact, I love it. Over and over in the pages that follow you'll see that I fit as many flavors and textures as possible into one place, from a little Parmesan crisp piled with cheese and sherried tomatoes to a seafood cocktail appetizer with not one but three types of shellfish, each with its own relish.

HOW TO USE THIS BOOK

I want this book to be as straightforward and user-friendly as the recipes themselves, so I've kept its organization fairly simple.

The following section, Basic Recipes, Equipment, and Jargon, is the stuff you might want to refer to from time to time, like my recipe for various stocks, my recommendation for what kind of grater to use, and what I mean when I say to "julienne" something or let something "rest" after cooking it.

Then we'll get right into the recipes. The book is organized the same way a steakhouse dinner is: drinks, cocktail food, salads and starters, soups, main courses and sides, sauces, and desserts. Have fun by mixing and matching these to your heart's content. The recipes are augmented by three features:

BREAK POINTS indicate times when you can stop cooking and come back to it an hour, a day, or even weeks later.

BONUS POINTS give an extra bit of information such as variations or other ways to use a component recipe.

TO DRINK At the back of the book we offer wine and beer suggestions, organized in a fun and easy-to-use chart. Rather than focusing exclusively on vintage-specific bottlings, a few wines are offered in each of eleven flavor and body profiles, such as Oaky/Full-Bodied White or Spicy Red. The wines in each category are organized as follows: Cheap and Clever, Above Average, and Cellar Selections. Beers are similarly profiled. The "To Drink" note at the end of each recipe refers to a corresponding flavor profile in these charts. In cooking with wine in recipes, I generally call for just a "dry white" or "full-flavored red" wine because a lot of the wine's characteristics are lost during cooking, leaving you with the acid of a white wine or the underlying sourness of a red, so a wide range of inexpensive choices is acceptable.

One more thing: Because steakhouse cooking is so closely associated with grilling, the introduction to Main Courses features a lot of grilling information. Ditto the information on purchasing steak on page 121. If you don't have a good butcher in your neighborhood, then you should find Meat by Mail, which is at the end, helpful as well.

BASIC RECIPES, EQUIPMENT, and JARGON

RECIPES

LEMON VINAIGRETTE

MAKES 1½ CUPS

Lemon vinaigrette is a real hero in my kitchen; it lifts the flavors of everything from chilled seafood to salads. Use it to dress cold, poached shellfish, or as a dipping sauce for shrimp. Lemons can vary in intensity depending on freshness, so you may need to add a few extra drops to get the desired lemony punch.

2 TABLESPOONS DIJON MUSTARD

¼ CUP FRESHLY SQUEEZED LEMON JUICE

1½ TEASPOONS MINCED FRESH THYME LEAVES

¾ CUP OLIVE OIL

KOSHER SALT

FRESHLY GROUND BLACK PEPPER

Put the mustard, lemon juice, and thyme in a blender and pulse just to incorporate. Set the blender at a medium speed and, with the motor running, pour in the oil gradually in a thin stream to make an emulsion. Season with 1 teaspoon salt and ½ teaspoon pepper, then thin by blending in 2 tablespoons cold water. If the mixture breaks while adding the water, just blend some more.

The vinaigrette can be covered and refrigerated for up to 3 days.

SHERRY VINAIGRETTE

MAKES ABOUT 1½ CUPS

More interesting than your basic red wine vinaigrette, sherry vinaigrette is a good, all-purpose salad dressing. This one is made with light brown sugar and thyme, which add sweetness and flavor.

¼ CUP DIJON MUSTARD

2 TABLESPOONS LIGHT BROWN SUGAR

¼ CUP SHERRY VINEGAR

1 TEASPOON MINCED FRESH THYME LEAVES

½ TEASPOON KOSHER SALT

¼ TEASPOON FRESHLY GROUND BLACK PEPPER

1 CUP OLIVE OIL

Put the mustard, brown sugar, vinegar, thyme, salt, and pepper in a blender and pulse just to incorporate. Set the blender at a low speed and, with the motor running, pour in the oil gradually in a thin stream to make an emulsion, then thin by blending in ¼ cup water. If the mixture breaks while adding the water, just blend some more. Transfer the vinaigrette to a small bowl, scraping down the sides of the blender with a rubber spatula.

The vinaigrette can be covered and refrigerated for up to 3 days.

VEGETABLE STOCK

MAKES 4 QUARTS

I think of vegetable stock as a middle ground between water and chicken or beef stock. It's often the best choice when you're cooking a vegetarian dish, or any dish in which water doesn't offer enough interest and a more potently flavored stock would distract from or overwhelm the other ingredients.

This recipe is very flexible; if you don't have all the ingredients, or the exact quantity of each, don't worry. So long as there's a good mix of white, green, and orange vegetables, you'll end up with the proper balance.

I FENNEL BULB, OR STEMS FROM 3 BULBS

I MEDIUM WHITE ONION, CUT INTO LARGE DICE

3 MEDIUM CARROTS, CUT INTO LARGE PIECES, OR PEELINGS FROM ABOUT 6 CARROTS

6 CELERY STALKS, CUT INTO LARGE PIECES

3 BAY LEAVES

4 FRESH THYME SPRIGS

I TABLESPOON BLACK PEPPERCORNS

4 FRESH FLAT-LEAF PARSLEY SPRIGS

2 TABLESPOONS KOSHER SALT

Put all of the ingredients in a heavy-bottomed soup pot or stock-pot. Add 4 quarts plus 2 cups cold water. Bring to a boil over high heat, then lower the heat and simmer for 15 to 20 minutes. Remove the pot from the heat and let steep for 45 minutes. Strain through a fine-mesh strainer set over a large bowl.

Use the stock right away; cool, cover, and refrigerate for up to 3 days; or freeze for up to 2 months.

CHICKEN STOCK

MAKES ABOUT 2 QUARTS

Chicken stock is probably the most frequently used stock in American kitchens. Here's my recipe for this essential ingredient in many sauces and soups. If you don't want to make your own stock, purchase a high-quality organic and/or low-sodium brand such as Pacific, Health Valley, or Kitchen Basics.

4 TO 5 POUNDS CHICKEN BONES (CHICKEN PARTS SUCH AS LEGS, THIGHS, AND WINGS CAN ALSO BE USED)

3 CELERY STALKS, ROUGHLY CHOPPED

1 MEDIUM CARROT, ROUGHLY CHOPPED

1 MEDIUM WHITE ONION, ROUGHLY CHOPPED

1 HEAD GARLIC, HALVED CROSSWISE

2 BAY LEAVES

3 FRESH THYME SPRIGS

2 TEASPOONS BLACK PEPPERCORNS

2 TEASPOONS KOSHER SALT

Put the chicken bones in a large pot and cover by 3 inches with cold water. Slowly bring the water to a boil over medium heat. Strain the chicken through a coarse-mesh strainer, rinsing off any scum that clings to the bones. Discard the liquid.

Return the chicken bones to the pot and cover them by 1 inch with cold water. Add the remaining ingredients, bring to a boil slowly over medium heat, then lower the heat and let simmer for 1½ hours, skimming any scum that rises to the surface.

Strain the stock and let it cool. Skim off any fat that rises to the surface.

Use the stock right away; cool, cover, and refrigerate for up to 3 days; or freeze for up to 2 months.

BONUS POINTS

To make a brown chicken stock, roast the bones, celery, carrot, onion, and garlic in a roasting pan at 400°F until browned, stirring occasionally, 40 to 45 minutes.

Remove the bones and vegetables from the roasting pan and transfer to a heavy-bottomed soup pot, discarding any fat that remains in the pan; if some fat adheres to the chicken pieces or vegetables, that's okay. Add the bay leaves, thyme, and peppercorns. Cover by 3 inches with cold water. Bring to a boil slowly over medium heat, then lower the heat and let simmer for 1½ hours, skimming any scum that rises to the surface.

Strain the stock into a clean pot. Bring to a boil over high heat and continue to boil until reduced by half (you will have about 1 quart stock) and slightly thickened, approximately 30 minutes. Season with the salt.

If using the stock right away, skim the fat from the surface with a kitchen spoon. Or cool, cover, and refrigerate for up to 3 days; or freeze for up to 2 months. If you refrigerate it, the fat will rise to the top and can be spooned off more easily at that point.

BEEF STOCK

MAKES ABOUT 3 QUARTS

There's just no substitute for a true, homemade beef stock in dishes that demand a full-blown, beefy flavor. If you don't want to make your own stock, purchase a high-quality organic and/or low-sodium brand such as Pacific, Health Valley, or Kitchen Basics.

3 POUNDS BEEF BONES

2 POUNDS VEAL SHANKS

2 MEDIUM WHITE ONIONS, ROUGHLY CHOPPED

4 CELERY STALKS, ROUGHLY CHOPPED

2 CARROTS, ROUGHLY CHOPPED

2 HEADS GARLIC, HALVED HORIZONTALLY

1/4 CUP TOMATO PASTE

3 FRESH THYME SPRIGS

2 BAY LEAVES

3/4 CUP RED WINE

Preheat the oven to 450°F.

Put the beef bones and veal shanks in a heavy-bottomed roasting pan and add the onions, celery, carrots, and garlic. Roast until very brown, stirring occasionally to brown all surfaces evenly, approximately 45 minutes. Add the tomato paste, thyme, and bay leaves. Stir to coat the other ingredients with the paste and cook for another 15 minutes.

Transfer the bones and vegetables to a large, heavy-bottomed soup pot. Discard any fat remaining in the pan and place the pan on the stovetop over medium heat. Add the red wine and stir to loosen any flavorful bits stuck to the bottom of the pan. Pour the liquid from the pan into the soup pot. Add 5 quarts water to the pot and bring to a boil over medium-high heat. Skim any foam from the surface and lower the heat. Let simmer for 5 to 6 hours, periodically skimming any scum that rises to the surface.

Remove the pot from the stove and strain through a fine-mesh strainer into another heavy-bottomed pot. Press on the solids with a wooden spoon to extract as much flavorful liquid as possible. Transfer the pot to the stove, bring to a boil, and continue to boil until reduced by about one-third.

If using the stock right away, skim the fat from the surface with a kitchen spoon. Or cool, cover, and refrigerate for up to 3 days; or freeze for up to 2 months. If you refrigerate or freeze, the fat will rise to the top and can be spooned off more easily at that point.

ROASTED GARLIC

Roasted garlic has become an indispensable staple of the modern American pantry. My peers and I use it to add a depth of flavor to sauces, soups, and even mashed potatoes.

2 HEADS GARLIC, UNPEELED, TOP THIRD CUT OFF AND DISCARDED

¼ CUP OLIVE OIL

KOSHER SALT

FRESHLY GROUND BLACK PEPPER

Preheat the oven to 325°F.

Put the garlic on a sheet of aluminum foil and drizzle with the olive oil. Season to taste with salt and pepper and seal the foil package. Roast until the cloves are tender to a knife tip, 35 to 40 minutes. Remove the packet from the oven and let cool. When cool enough to handle, squeeze the individual cloves out of the papery skins.

To make a roasted garlic puree for stirring into liquids, mash the cloves with a fork or chop and flatten them with a knife.

The roasted garlic cloves, whole or pureed, can be covered and refrigerated for up to 2 days.

ROASTED TOMATOES

MAKES ABOUT ½ CUP

This is another go-to ingredient that modern American chefs use to punctuate a wide range of dishes with sweet and tangy flavor.

4 PLUM TOMATOES

3 TABLESPOONS EXTRA VIRGIN OLIVE OIL

3 GARLIC CLOVES, THINLY SLICED

4 FRESH THYME SPRIGS

Preheat the oven to 325°F.

Core and split the tomatoes and arrange them in a single layer in a roasting pan or on a Silpat-lined baking sheet. Drizzle with the olive oil and scatter the garlic and thyme over them. Roast until lightly browned and slightly dehydrated, approximately 40 minutes. When cool enough to handle, remove the skins and roughly chop the tomatoes.

CLARIFIED BUTTER

MAKES 1½ CUPS

Clarified butter is an essential component of Hollandaise sauce (page 185) and its variations, and is often brushed on cooked steaks. On its own, it's a great, easy pairing for cooked lobster.

1 POUND (4 STICKS) UNSALTED BUTTER

Put the butter in a small pot over medium heat, melt, and bring to a simmer. Skim the milk solids that rise to the top and discard them. Continue to skim until no more milk solids rise to the surface. Strain the butter through a fine-mesh sieve.

The butter can be cooled, covered, and refrigerated for up to 3 days.

BREAD CRUMB TOPPING

MAKES ABOUT ¾ CUP

I use this breading to top baked and roasted tomatoes and vegetables. Its combination of herbs, lemon zest, olive oil, and salt coaxes the flavor out of whatever you put it on.

½ CUP PANKO (JAPANESE BREAD CRUMBS)

½ TEASPOON MINCED FRESH THYME LEAVES

½ TEASPOON MINCED FRESH ROSEMARY LEAVES

½ TEASPOON FINELY GRATED LEMON ZEST

2 TABLESPOONS EXTRA VIRGIN OLIVE OIL

½ TEASPOON KOSHER SALT

Mix all the ingredients together in a small bowl.

EQUIPMENT

There's no end to the equipment you can buy for your home kitchen, but for the recipes in this book, the following are really essential.

FOR GENERAL COOKING

BOWLS. I find it very helpful to have a selection of ceramic, glass, and stainless-steel bowls in various sizes.

CUTTING BOARD. You should have at least one very thick, sturdy cutting board and keep it scrupulously clean by washing with hot water and antibacterial soap after every use, and immediately after cutting raw fish and poultry. To help keep it from sliding around, always put a damp paper towel under it. This is one of the first things they teach you in cooking school and it alone is almost worth the tuition.

GRATERS. Microplane graters are a relatively new addition to the equipment check list, based on a woodworking tool with hundreds of tiny blades that has become a standard piece of equipment in modern kitchens. It's really the only way to grate things like lemon zest and hard cheeses, both of which you'll be doing a lot as you cook from this book.

IMMERSION BLENDER. Immersion blenders, also known as hand blenders, are lightweight, motorized wands with a blending blade at the end; they allow you to save a step by blending right in the pot. They're not essential, but once you try one, you might never use your standing blender again.

KNIVES. I believe that it's almost impossible to have too many knives. In fact, I have specific knives for specific tasks, like slicing tomatoes. (Maybe it's because I'm a recreational golfer who's used to using one club to tee off, one to putt, and one to chip out of sand traps and the like.) The selection of a knife is very personal and subjective. One major consideration is that knives are made from many types of steel. For many cooks, stainless-steel knives are the way to go because of their versatility; carbon knives can throw off the color of acidic foods like onions and tomatoes. Generally speaking, I'm a big fan of the very sharp but inexpensive line of Forschner knives.

MANDOLINE. The very sharp flat blades and removable "teeth" blades of these manual slicing machines are essential to making very precise cuts, especially very thin ones, and for making strips from carrots, potatoes, cucumbers, and other vegetables. I recommend a Japanese Benriner because of its razor-sharp cutting blades. When using a mandoline, be sure to protect your hands and work slowly.

PASTRY BAG. Whether for decorating a cake or piping whipped cheese onto Parmesan crisps, a pastry bag is a useful thing to have in your kitchen, and so cheap that there's really no reason not to.

SILPAT (NONSTICK BAKING MAT). More convenient, durable, and user-friendly than wax paper, a Silpat doesn't burn and ensures consistent heat transfer from the baking sheet to the food. I use these mats for making cheese crisps, roasting tomatoes, and working with puff pastry.

SPICE MILL OR COFFEE GRINDER. I believe in grinding spices as you use them, when possible. This is always true of black pepper, which should be kept in its own mill. But I often like to freshly grind other spices for the increased freshness of flavor. If you don't already own one, get yourself an extra mill or a small, electric coffee grinder that can be used for different spices. Be sure to brush it out between spices to keep unwanted flavors from lingering.

STRAINERS. Most home cooks have one fine-mesh strainer that gets used for all draining or straining. I strongly urge you to add a variety of mesh strainers to your collection. At the very least you should have a fine-mesh strainer, a coarse-mesh strainer, and a colander. Straining, say, soups often calls for a different type of strainer than straining sauces. Have enough choices on hand to get the exact result called for by each dish.

THERMOMETERS. There are two thermometers you simply must have. One is an instant-read meat thermometer. The other is a clip-on oil or candy thermometer. When you need to remove a piece of meat from the heat or start frying in oil at an exact temperature, there's simply no other way to be accurate. Variables like oven calibration, conductivity and thickness of pans, and starting temperature all influence the rate at which foods and oils cook or heat up.

THICK-GAUGE, FLAT BAKING SHEETS. Flat baking sheets, preferably with a rimmed edge for catching juices, are useful for baking and roasting everything from vegetables to puff pastry. I like a 12 by 19-inch sheet for oven use and smaller, stainless-steel trays measuring 12 by 10 inches for holding prepared ingredients. I find them more user-friendly than ramekins or other vessels.

FOR GRILLING

HEAVY-DUTY, BRASS GRILL BRUSH. A must. You really need to regularly brush off any cooked-on food from the grill grate.

SPATULA. A spatula is more useful at the grill than you might think because grilling can soften ingredients like fish and tender vegetables to the point where tongs can break or mar them. That's when you need a spatula for turning and moving. Select one with a weight and balance that feel good in your hand and will give you the support to control heavy foods if necessary. They come perforated and solid. I own one of each. The solid one is good for moving delicate items like fruit off the grill; the perforated is better for lifting off burgers and steaks, allowing excess grease to run right off.

TONGS. Another must. Restaurant-quality, by which I mean heavy-duty, stainless-steel cooking tongs, give you the control and confidence to deftly move, turn, and remove meats and vegetables on the grill. There are different-length tongs on the market; choose one at least 9 inches long to let you stay at a minimal safe distance from the flame.

JARGON

There are some words I use throughout this book that you may not be familiar with. Some of them are unique to a professional kitchen, some are unique to grilling, and some are my own little words that I think are very descriptive.

FOLD. To fold ingredients into one another means to gently combine them (rather than vigorously beating them) with broad strokes, usually with a rubber spatula.

JULIENNE. To thinly slice an ingredient, usually a vegetable, into $\frac{1}{16}$ by $1\frac{1}{2}$- to 2-inch strips. The length of ingredients julienned for the same dish should be uniform.

MINCE. Mince means to finely chop an ingredient in no particular shape. Don't confuse it with "finely dicing," which means to carefully slice an ingredient into little cubes.

PEG. Peg isn't a standard-issue kitchen word but I find it to be a very descriptive way of referring to $\frac{1}{4}$-inch strips of vegetables, measuring about 3 inches in length, or shorter if the vegetable itself is smaller. I generally use it with tomatoes, peppers, and onions.

PULSE. Pulse refers to chopping an ingredient, or ingredients, in a food processor by briefly pressing the on button several times rather than simply letting the motor run. It's usually used to process something just enough rather than pulverizing or liquefying it.

PULVERIZE. I frequently refer to pulverizing garlic. To do this, use the side of a large, heavy knife to smash a peeled clove (or cloves), sprinkle it with a pinch of salt, and continue to press on and mash the garlic to turn it into a paste. If using more garlic, add more salt accordingly.

REST. Allowing a piece of meat to rest after cooking isn't done to cool it off. When meat rests, the juices, which are driven to the center of the meat during cooking, have a chance to redistribute, ensuring a more desirable flavor and texture throughout. This time also allows for "carryover" cooking, during which the heat contained by the meat continues to cook it.

DRINKS

Standards and Surprises to Get Things Started

The first question I ask each guest in my home is the same one that the waitstaff poses at my steakhouses: "What can I get you to drink?"

Offering a drink is a universal gesture of hospitality, a welcome to the festivities and a harbinger of good things to come. Drinks are never dictated; even at home, where there's a set lunch or dinner menu, there's always a choice of what will be poured into your glass.

The drinks in this chapter were selected in that spirit. There's something for everyone, from classics like Whiskey Sour (page 26) and Rob Roy (page 25) to modern masterpieces like Cosmopolitan (page 29) and Flirtini (page 29).

As a nod to the diverse tastes present in a home, as well as the fact that there may be children in attendance, I've also included several nonalcoholic beverages such as Berry Lemonade (page 31) and Ginger-Raspberry Iced Tea (page 32).

My favorite entry in this chapter is the Make-Your-Own-Martini Bar (page 27), which has many of the same appealing elements as the food recipes in the book, allowing you to prepare it in advance while still factoring in the distinct desires of each guest.

All recipes can be multiplied to make more servings at a time.

CLASSIC COCKTAILS

Even though this book is devoted to New American steakhouse cooking, there are a few classic cocktails that I simply had to share. Unlike today's cocktails, many of which are based primarily on flavor, many classics were inspired and named for specific spirit combinations, such as the Gin Fizz and Whiskey Sour.

GIN FIZZ

SERVES I

¼ CUP GIN

JUICE OF ½ LEMON

I TEASPOON CONFECTIONERS' SUGAR

CLUB SODA

Put ice in a cocktail shaker, and put 2 ice cubes in a highball glass. Pour the gin and lemon juice into the shaker, add the sugar, shake, and strain into the glass. Fill with club soda, stir, and serve.

ROB ROY

SERVES I

1½ TABLESPOONS SWEET VERMOUTH

3 TABLESPOONS SCOTCH

Put ice in a cocktail shaker. Add the vermouth and Scotch, stir, and strain into a cocktail glass.

SHANDY

SERVES I

¼ CUP PILSNER

¼ CUP GINGER ALE

Fill a tall glass with ice. Pour the pilsner and ginger ale over the ice, gently stir, and serve.

STINGER

SERVES 1

1½ TABLESPOONS WHITE CRÈME DE
MENTHE

¼ CUP BRANDY

Put ice in a cocktail shaker. Add the crème de menthe and brandy, shake, and strain into a martini glass.

WHISKEY SOUR

SERVES 1

JUICE OF ½ LEMON

1½ TEASPOONS CONFECTIONERS'
SUGAR

¼ CUP BLENDED WHISKEY SUCH AS
JOHNNIE WALKER BLACK LABEL,
DEWARS, OR CUTTY SARK

1 THIN SLICE LEMON OR LIME

1 MARASCHINO CHERRY

Put ice cubes in a cocktail shaker. Add the lemon juice, sugar, and whiskey. Shake and strain into a cocktail glass. Garnish with the lemon or lime slice and cherry.

MAKE-YOUR-OWN-MARTINI BAR

There's nothing like a martini to set the stage for a steakhouse dinner. This most classic of cocktails is both simple and complex. There are just a few ground rules—gin and vermouth served ice-cold—but the variations are endless: the first and most forgotten example being vodka, which, while not the traditional choice, has become as popular as gin in the martini, at least in the United States.

If you're a martini drinker or know a few, then you know that everyone has his or her own preferred version: dry or neat, straight up or on the rocks, dirty (with some olive brine added) or not. And, of course, there's the "James Bond" question (shaken or stirred?). And, finally, whether to garnish it with olives or a lemon twist.

You've got enough things to worry about when you're making dinner for guests; you don't need to be shaking and stirring a different martini for everyone. My solution is to set up a martini bar so guests can create their own martinis. It's fun and different and people love it.

EQUIPMENT

12- to 24-ounce martini shaker, with a strainer top or a separate strainer (if using one without a strainer top you'll need a mixing glass that fits snuggly inside the shaker to keep the drink from leaking when shaking it)

1-ounce jigger

Ceramic cruet or small pitcher, to serve olive brine for "dirty" martinis

8- to 10-ounce martini glasses

Ice bowl

INGREDIENTS

Super-premium vodka such as Ketel One, Belvedere, or Chopin (the more brands, the better)

Spanish olives and olive brine

Dry vermouth

Ice

THE **PERFECT STRIP HOUSE**
DIRTY VODKA MARTINI

SERVES 1

1½ TABLESPOONS DRY VERMOUTH

7 TABLESPOONS, OR ½ CUP MINUS
1 TABLESPOON PREMIUM VODKA

3 LARGE SPANISH OLIVES

OLIVE BRINE

Fill a shaker three-quarters full with ice cubes. Pour in the dry vermouth and gently shake once or twice to coat the ice cubes with vermouth. Strain the vermouth from the strainer and discard, leaving the ice in the shaker. Pour in the vodka and shake vigorously about five times. Strain this into a chilled martini glass. Add the olives to the glass and serve the olive brine in a cruet on the side for guests to season their martinis to taste.

BONUS POINTS
Give your guests more to choose from with flavored vodkas like pepper and lemon and a variety of garnishes such as pickled jalapeños, tomolives (cherry tomatoes pickled like olives), or lime twists.

CONTEMPORARY COCKTAILS

It's no accident that three of the following four cocktails are made with the flavorless spirit vodka. Many masterpieces of modern mixology are based on a combination of vibrantly flavored fruit juices, making vodka the perfect choice.

COSMOPOLITAN

SERVES 1

3 TABLESPOONS PREMIUM VODKA

1½ TEASPOONS FRESHLY SQUEEZED LIME JUICE PLUS 1 LIME WEDGE

1½ TEASPOONS TRIPLE SEC

1½ TEASPOONS CRANBERRY JUICE

Put 1 cup ice cubes in a shaker. Add the vodka, lime juice, triple sec, and cranberry juice. Shake and strain into a martini glass. Garnish with the lime wedge.

FLIRTINI

SERVES 1

3 TABLESPOONS PLUS 1 TEASPOON PREMIUM VODKA

1 TABLESPOON COINTREAU

2 TABLESPOONS PINEAPPLE JUICE

3 TABLESPOONS CHAMPAGNE, PLUS SOME FOR FLOATER

Put ½ cup ice cubes in a cocktail shaker. Add the vodka, Cointreau, pineapple juice, and Champagne. Shake and strain into a martini glass. Top with a floater of Champagne, filling the glass to the rim.

STRIP HOUSE
SUMMERTIME COOLER

SERVES 2

½ CUP MYERS'S DARK RUM

½ CUP WHOLE RASPBERRIES
(ABOUT 20 BERRIES)

¼ CUP CRANBERRY JUICE

2 TABLESPOONS FRESHLY SQUEEZED
LEMON JUICE

I LEMON, CUT INTO 6 WEDGES

6 FRESH MINT LEAVES

I TABLESPOON SUPERFINE SUGAR

Put ¾ cup ice cubes in a shaker. Add all the ingredients, shake well, and divide between 2 highball glasses, ice cubes and all.

URBANITE

SERVES I

2 TABLESPOONS PASSION FRUIT JUICE

3 TABLESPOONS GRAPEFRUIT JUICE

2 TABLESPOONS PINEAPPLE JUICE

¼ CUP PREMIUM VODKA

Put ½ cup ice cubes in a shaker. Add all the ingredients, shake, and strain into a martini glass.

NONALCOHOLIC DRINKS

You don't have to be a kid to appreciate these alcohol-free drinks. They're just as appealing to adults, whether as an alternative to a "real" cocktail or a break between them. They also go great with the dishes in this book, from cocktail food to main courses and sides.

BERRY LEMONADE

SERVES 4

½ CUP RASPBERRIES
(ABOUT 20 BERRIES)

½ CUP BLACKBERRIES
(ABOUT 16 BERRIES)

¾ CUP SUPERFINE SUGAR

2 CUPS FRESHLY SQUEEZED LEMON
JUICE (FROM ABOUT 30 LEMONS)

1 CUP ORANGE JUICE

2 LEMONS, THINLY SLICED

Put 3 cups ice cubes in a pitcher. Add 1 cup water, the raspberries, blackberries, sugar, and lemon juice. Stir well to break down the berries. Add the orange juice and lemons and chill before serving.

ICED GREEN TEA
WITH MINT AND LIME

SERVES 4

¼ CUP SUGAR

6 GREEN TEA BAGS

¼ CUP FRESH MINT LEAVES

1½ TEASPOONS FRESHLY SQUEEZED
LIME JUICE

Put ¼ cup water in a small, heavy-bottomed pot and add the sugar. Bring to a boil over high heat, then remove the pot from the heat.

Pour 3¾ cups water into a separate pot and bring to a boil over high heat. Remove the pot from the heat, add the tea bags and mint, and let steep for 5 to 6 minutes. Add the lime juice, 1 cup ice cubes, and the simple syrup. Let chill. Serve in ice-filled tumblers.

GINGER-RASPBERRY
ICED TEA

SERVES 4

1/4 CUP PEELED, ROUGHLY CHOPPED
FRESH GINGER

1/4 CUP FRESH RASPBERRIES

5 ENGLISH BREAKFAST TEA BAGS

Put the ginger, raspberries, and 1/2 cup water in a food processor fitted with the steel blade. Puree until the ginger is finely ground. Squeeze the mixture in cheesecloth and reserve the ginger-raspberry juice. Discard the solids.

Bring 3 1/2 cups water to a boil in a pot over high heat. Remove from the heat and add the ginger-raspberry juice and the tea bags. Let steep for 30 minutes. Remove bags. Fill a pitcher with ice cubes and pour in the ginger tea. Serve cold.

PASSION FRUIT FLOAT

SERVES 1

1/2 CUP VANILLA ICE CREAM
(ABOUT 2 SMALL SCOOPS)

1/4 CUP PASSION FRUIT JUICE
(SEE PAGE 193)

1/4 CUP COCONUT MILK

1/4 CUP SELTZER WATER

Put the ice cream in a large, bowl-shaped glass. Add the remaining ingredients and serve.

COCKTAIL FOOD

Small Stuff to Pass Around the Room or Table

You won't find the phrase "cocktail food" in the dictionary, but everybody knows what it means. Cocktail food is food that's meant to be passed around a room or shared at the table during the early stages of a get-together. It's food that goes great with beer, wine, and/or mixed drinks. It satisfies the mouth but doesn't kill the appetite. It's what my parents' generation called hors d'oeuvres, but which my generation of chefs have Americanized, inspiring me to call the category by an American name.

I've developed a huge repertoire of cocktail food in the restaurants where I've worked, from the southwestern Tapika, where I first introduced what I call "table-share appetizers" on the menu, to the many steakhouses where I'm the chef today.

I think that cocktail food is very important, not just something to have out when people arrive. To me, cocktail food sets the tone for an evening with microbites that are a little preview of things to come.

This chapter features a cross section of my favorite cocktail food, including vegetarian, fish, poultry, and meat. They all pass my checklist of musts:

- They can be made, at least partially, in advance. When entertaining, anything that can be done ahead of time gets a gold star next to it because it makes your life easier. All of these recipes receive that extra credit.

- They pack a ton of flavor into a small space. I love cocktail food that demands to be noticed. So I try to fit more flavors in each bite, or on each plate, than you may expect.

- They're drink-friendly. If you're going to call a chapter "Cocktail Food," you better be offering up recipes that belong next to a beer, a glass of wine, or a cocktail.

- They're fun to eat. My favorite cocktail foods are the ones that you pick up with your fingers and the ultimate ones are those that get dunked in a sauce on their way to your mouth. There's a lot of dunking here.

VEGETABLE ROLL
WITH **GINGER–GREEN CHILE SAUCE**

SERVES 4 TO 6 (MAKES 4 ROLLS, 24 TO 32 BITE-SIZE PIECES)

Make-ahead cocktail food doesn't get much better than this. These rolls don't even ask you to do much cooking: you just turn on the stove for a few seconds to soften up the tortillas. Marinating the raw vegetables in lemon vinaigrette breaks them down and integrates their flavors just as a quick sauté would, but with a minimum of oil, so they taste clean and fresh.

I take vegetable rolls in a southwestern direction with flour tortillas. These also call on one of my favorite go-to flavor tricks—flicking an assortment of herbs over the vegetables to create surprising bursts of flavor that vary from bite to bite.

I CARROT, JULIENNED

2 CELERY STALKS, SCRAPED OF FIBROUS EXTERIOR AND JULIENNED

2 CUPS VERY THINLY SLICED WHITE CABBAGE (FROM ABOUT 1/3 HEAD CABBAGE)

I ZUCCHINI, JULIENNED FROM THE SKIN TO THE SEEDS, SEEDS DISCARDED

I RED BELL PEPPER, VERY THINLY SLICED LENGTHWISE

3/4 CUP LEMON VINAIGRETTE (PAGE II)

KOSHER SALT

FRESHLY GROUND BLACK PEPPER

4 FLOUR TORTILLAS, IO INCHES IN DIAMETER

I BUNCH FRESH CHIVES

8 FRESH MINT LEAVES

8 FRESH CILANTRO SPRIGS

8 FRESH BASIL LEAVES, EACH TORN IN HALF

GINGER–GREEN CHILE SAUCE (RECIPE FOLLOWS)

Put the carrot, celery, cabbage, zucchini, and bell pepper in a bowl. Drizzle with the vinaigrette, season with 1/4 teaspoon salt and 1/4 teaspoon pepper, and toss. Let stand for 15 to 20 minutes at room temperature; during this time, the vegetables will begin to soften and break down.

Transfer the vegetables to a clean bowl, gently squeezing out most of the vinaigrette and juice by hand; you want to remove most of the liquid without crushing the shape out of the vegetables. Discard the liquid.

Warm a tortilla over a gas flame, or in a hot dry skillet set over high heat, until pliable, 20 to 30 seconds. Set aside on a plate and repeat with the remaining tortillas.

Lay 1 tortilla on a work surface and spoon one-quarter of the vegetables in a neat, cigar-shaped column down the center. Scatter one-quarter of the chives, mint, cilantro, and basil randomly over the vegetables. Roll the tortilla tautly around the vegetables, brush some ginger-chile sauce along the edge to "glue" it closed, then finish rolling it. Set the roll, seam side down, on a clean plate.

Repeat with the remaining tortillas, vegetables, and herbs.

(CONTINUED)

The rolls can be made to this point, individually wrapped in plastic wrap, and refrigerated for 3 to 4 hours. Serve them cold or at room temperature.

To serve, cut each roll into 1-inch pieces and arrange the pieces on a large plate or platter. Pour the remaining sauce into a ramekin or small bowl and set in the middle of the platter. Let everyone dip their pieces into the sauce.

GINGER–GREEN CHILE SAUCE

MAKES 1½ CUPS

4 OUNCES PEELED FRESH GINGER (ONE 5- TO 6-INCH-LONG KNOB), ROUGHLY CHOPPED

2 TABLESPOONS FRESHLY SQUEEZED LIME JUICE

¼ CUP SLICED PICKLED JALAPEÑOS

½ CUP MAYONNAISE

KOSHER SALT

FRESHLY GROUND BLACK PEPPER

TO DRINK
CRISP/FRESH WHITE
LIGHT-BODIED BEER

Put the ginger, lime juice, jalapeños, and 2 tablespoons water in a food processor fitted with the steel blade or in a standing blender. Puree to a paste. Pour the mixture onto a sheet of cheesecloth, roll up the cloth, and squeeze over a small bowl to extract the liquid. Discard the solids. Whisk in the mayonnaise and season with ¼ teaspoon salt and ¼ teaspoon pepper. Cover and refrigerate until ready to use.

The sauce can be covered and refrigerated for up to 2 days.

WHIPPED GARLIC GOAT CHEESE
AND **SHERRIED TOMATOES** ON **CHEESE CRISPS**

SERVES 4 TO 6 (MAKES 40 PIECES)

These crisps answer the question "How many flavors can fit in the same small space?" Herbs, garlic, goat cheese, sherry vinegar, tomatoes, and Parmigiano-Reggiano cheese are piled one on top of another. When you pop the crisp in your mouth, the flavors just keep coming—pow, pow, pow—each one complementing all the others. You might want to make double the amount here; people tend to wolf these down.

Cheese crisps usually turn up as perfectly shaped tuiles, but I like to bake all of the Parmigiano-Reggiano together in a sheet and break it up into little abstract pieces. If you don't have a pastry bag, break the crisps into slightly larger pieces and use two teaspoons to apply the cheese and tomatoes, scooping the ingredients up with one teaspoon and pushing them onto the crisps with the other.

2 CUPS FINELY GRATED PARMIGIANO-REGGIANO CHEESE (FROM ABOUT 8 OUNCES CHEESE)

8 OUNCES GOAT CHEESE, SOFTENED AT ROOM TEMPERATURE

I GARLIC CLOVE, MINCED, PLUS 3 GARLIC CLOVES, THINLY SLICED

2 TABLESPOONS THINLY SLICED FRESH CHIVES

1/2 TEASPOON MINCED FRESH THYME LEAVES

1/4 TEASPOON MINCED FRESH ROSEMARY LEAVES

1/2 TEASPOON FINELY GRATED LEMON ZEST

KOSHER SALT

FRESHLY GROUND BLACK PEPPER

1/4 CUP EXTRA VIRGIN OLIVE OIL

1/4 CUP SHERRY VINEGAR

4 PLUM TOMATOES, PEELED (SEE NOTE), SEEDED, AND CUT INTO VERY SMALL DICE

2 FRESH BASIL LEAVES, VERY THINLY SLICED

Preheat the oven to 350°F.

Spread the Parmigiano-Reggiano on a nonstick baking sheet and shape into a rectangle about 9 inches wide, 13 inches long, and 1/8 inch thick. Bake until golden brown, approximately 15 minutes. Remove the sheet from the oven and let the cheese cool to room temperature. The cheese will be brittle; break it into small pieces about 1/2 inch across.

BREAK POINT
The cheese crisps can be made up to 24 hours ahead of time and kept in an airtight container at room temperature.

Put the goat cheese, minced garlic, chives, thyme, rosemary, lemon zest, 1/4 teaspoon salt, and 1/4 teaspoon pepper in the bowl of a standing mixer and whip until the ingredients are well integrated into a whipped herb cheese. (Or do this in a regular mixing bowl and use a handheld mixer.) Transfer the mixture to a pastry bag fitted with the star tip, scraping down the sides of the bowl with a rubber spatula. Set aside at room temperature.

(CONTINUED)

8 FRESH CHERVIL SPRIGS

TO DRINK
OAKY/FULL-BODIED WHITE ROSÉ

BREAK POINT
The whipped cheese can be covered and refrigerated for up to 24 hours. Let soften at room temperature for about 30 minutes before proceeding.

Heat the oil in a heavy-bottomed saucepan over high heat. Add the sliced garlic and cook until lightly browned, approximately 1 minute. Add the vinegar and tomatoes, stir, then add the basil, ½ teaspoon salt, and ¼ teaspoon pepper and stir again. Cook for another 10 seconds, then remove the pan from the heat and let the mixture cool. Cover and refrigerate until cold.

BREAK POINT
The tomato mixture can be refrigerated for up to 2 hours, but no longer. Drain the tomatoes before proceeding.

To serve, pipe some whipped cheese onto each crisp. Top each one with a dollop of sherried tomatoes. Garnish with the chervil and serve.

Note: To Peel Tomatoes
Bring a large pot of water to a boil over high heat. Fill a large bowl halfway with ice water. Core the tomatoes and slice a shallow X in the skin at the bottom. Add the tomatoes to the boiling water and cook just until the skin begins to pull away at the edges of the X, 15 to 20 seconds, then immediately (you don't want the tomatoes to soften at all), use tongs or a slotted spoon to transfer the tomatoes to the ice water. When cool enough to handle, peel and discard the tomatoes' skin. If it doesn't come right off, use a paring knife to loosen it.

ICED JUMBO SHRIMP COCKTAIL
WITH **HOMEMADE COCKTAIL SAUCE**

SERVES 6

This shrimp cocktail is a prime example of how much difference a few well-chosen ingredients can make. The fresh garlic and tomatoes in the sauce and the fact that you can doctor it to taste just might make it the best one you've ever had. If you can, make the cocktail sauce a day in advance and chill it in the refrigerator to really maximize the flavors.

1½ POUNDS JUMBO SHRIMP (ABOUT 24 SHRIMP)

1 CUP DRY WHITE WINE

2 LEMONS, THINLY SLICED

4 FRESH THYME SPRIGS

1 HEAD GARLIC, HALVED CROSSWISE

6 FRESH FLAT-LEAF PARSLEY SPRIGS

KOSHER SALT

1 TABLESPOON CORIANDER SEEDS

1 TABLESPOON BLACK PEPPERCORNS

COCKTAIL SAUCE (PAGE 173)

TO DRINK
LIGHT/FLORAL WHITE
AMBER BEER

Peel the shell from each shrimp, leaving the tail and last segment of shell intact. One by one, lay the shrimp on a clean surface on their sides and slice the back of the shrimp slightly. Rinse the shrimp under cold water to remove any black impurities inside the back of the shrimp. As they are cleaned, gather the shrimp in a bowl; cover and refrigerate until ready to cook.

Pour 2 quarts water into a large, heavy-bottomed pot and add the wine, lemons, thyme, garlic, parsley, 2 tablespoons salt, coriander, and peppercorns. Bring to a boil over high heat. Fill a large bowl with ice water.

When the water boils, add the shrimp and poach until firm and pink, 2½ to 3 minutes. Use a slotted spoon to transfer the shrimp to the ice water to stop the cooking quickly. Spread the shrimp out on a baking sheet and pick off and discard any herbs and lemon pieces. Cover the shrimp with plastic wrap and chill in the refrigerator for at least 2 hours.

BREAK POINT
The shrimp can be prepared to this point and refrigerated for up to 24 hours.

To serve, put a small bowl in the center of a chilled serving platter and surround it with a shallow layer of crushed ice. Pour the cocktail sauce into the bowl and arrange the shrimp on the ice.

SEEFOOD COCKTAIL
WITH **THREE RELISHES**

SERVES 6

Here's another dish that lives by my rule of "the more flavors, the merrier," provided of course that they get along with and build on one another. Three varieties of cooked shellfish, each matched with its own relish, provide an assortment of mix-and-match possibilities on one plate. Plan a bit ahead to make this, as the relishes must cool for at least two hours.

¼ CUP CORN OIL OR OTHER NEUTRAL OIL SUCH AS GRAPESEED OR CANOLA

10 OUNCES CLEANED BABY SQUID, FROM ABOUT 1 POUND UNCLEANED SQUID, CUT INTO ½-INCH RINGS

2 TABLESPOONS UNSALTED BUTTER

KOSHER SALT

FRESHLY GROUND BLACK PEPPER

1 POUND JUMBO SEA SCALLOPS (10 TO 12 SCALLOPS), PREFERABLY DRY-PACKED

CELERY-FENNEL RELISH (RECIPE FOLLOWS)

YELLOW PEPPER RELISH (RECIPE FOLLOWS)

TOMATO-ZUCCHINI RELISH (RECIPE FOLLOWS)

8 OUNCES JUMBO LUMP CRABMEAT, PICKED FREE OF SHELL FRAGMENTS, CHILLED

TO DRINK
CRISP/FRESH WHITE
BLOND BEER

Heat 2 tablespoons of the oil in a small, heavy-bottomed sauté pan set over medium heat. Add the cut squid and cook until white, 3 to 4 minutes. Toss in 1 tablespoon of the butter and heat until melted, then season with ½ teaspoon salt and a pinch of pepper.

Remove the pan from the heat and let the squid cool slightly. Transfer the squid to an airtight container and chill in the refrigerator for at least 2 hours or up to 24 hours.

Wipe out the pan and heat the remaining 2 tablespoons oil in the pan over medium heat. Add the scallops to the pan in 2 batches and sauté on each side until a deep golden brown, 2 to 3 minutes per side. (Do this in batches even if you have a very large pan; adding all of the scallops at once will cool the pan down and keep them from searing properly.)

As they are done, transfer the scallops to a paper-towel-lined plate.

When all of the scallops are sautéed, add the remaining 1 table-spoon butter to the pan and swirl it around as it melts. Add 1 tablespoon salt and 1 teaspoon pepper to the butter and pour the butter mixture over the sautéed scallops.

To serve, dollop 2 tablespoons of each relish in the center of a serving plate; put the squid on top of the Celery-Fennel Relish, the scallops on the Yellow Pepper Relish, and the crabmeat on the Tomato-Zucchini Relish. Or put the chilled seafood in individual bowls and serve the relishes alongside the appropriate seafood.

CELERY-FENNEL RELISH

MAKES 1¼ CUPS

2 TABLESPOONS UNSALTED BUTTER

½ CUP FINELY DICED WHITE ONIONS

1 CUP FINELY DICED FENNEL

1 CUP FINELY DICED CELERY

¼ CUP ANISETTE LIQUEUR OR SAMBUCA

3 TABLESPOONS LIGHT BROWN SUGAR

½ TEASPOON GROUND FENNEL SEEDS

1 TEASPOON CHOPPED FRESH TARRAGON LEAVES

KOSHER SALT

2 TABLESPOONS CORN SYRUP

¼ CUP FRESHLY SQUEEZED LEMON JUICE

4 LONG STRIPS LEMON PEEL, REMOVED WITH A VEGETABLE PEELER, EACH ABOUT ½ INCH WIDE

½ TEASPOON CRACKED BLACK PEPPER

Melt the butter in a medium, heavy-bottomed pot over medium heat. Add the onions, diced fennel, and celery and sauté until softened but not browned, 4 to 5 minutes. Remove the pot from the heat, lean away, and add the anisette. Carefully return the pot to the flame, still leaning away from it, and let the anisette ignite and burn until the alcohol cooks off.

Add the sugar, fennel seeds, tarragon, 1 teaspoon salt, corn syrup, lemon juice and peel, and pepper to the pot and cook over medium-low heat, stirring, until reduced and thickened, 15 to 20 minutes. Remove the pot from the heat, let the mixture cool, pick out and discard the lemon peel, then cover and refrigerate for at least 2 hours or up to 24 hours.

YELLOW PEPPER RELISH

MAKES 1¼ CUPS

2 CUPS FINELY DICED YELLOW BELL PEPPERS (FROM ABOUT 2 BELL PEPPERS)

½ CUP FINELY DICED WHITE ONIONS

2 TEASPOONS PEELED, MINCED FRESH GINGER (ABOUT 1-INCH SECTION)

½ CUP DISTILLED WHITE VINEGAR

½ CUP CORN SYRUP

1½ TEASPOONS CURRY POWDER

¼ TEASPOON GROUND CLOVES

2 CINNAMON STICKS

½ TEASPOON CRUSHED RED PEPPER FLAKES

3 BAY LEAVES

1 TEASPOON KOSHER SALT

Bring all of the ingredients to a simmer in a medium saucepan over medium heat. Continue to simmer until very thick, 20 to 25 minutes. Remove the pan from the heat and let the mixture cool, then cover and refrigerate for at least 2 hours or up to 24 hours.

(CONTINUED)

TOMATO-ZUCCHINI RELISH

MAKES 1 1/4 CUPS

1 TABLESPOON CORN OR OTHER
NEUTRAL OIL SUCH AS GRAPESEED
OR CANOLA

1/4 CUP DICED WHITE ONION

2 GARLIC CLOVES, THINLY SLICED

1 CUP DICED PLUM TOMATOES (FROM
ABOUT 3 TOMATOES)

3/4 CUP DICED ZUCCHINI (FROM ABOUT
10 OUNCES ZUCCHINI)

1 TEASPOON TOMATO PASTE

1 TABLESPOON RED WINE VINEGAR

2 TABLESPOONS CORN SYRUP

1 1/2 TEASPOONS CHOPPED FRESH
BASIL LEAVES

KOSHER SALT

FRESHLY GROUND BLACK PEPPER

1/2 TEASPOON GRATED LEMON ZEST

Heat the oil in a heavy-bottomed saucepan over medium heat. Add the onion and garlic and sauté until softened but not browned, approximately 4 minutes.

Add the tomatoes and zucchini and cook over medium heat, stirring to prevent scorching, for 4 to 5 minutes. Add the tomato paste and stir to coat the other ingredients with the paste. Add the vinegar, corn syrup, basil, 1/2 teaspoon salt, 1/4 teaspoon pepper, and lemon zest and cook, stirring, until nicely thickened, 6 to 8 minutes.

Remove the pan from the heat and let the mixture cool, then cover and refrigerate for at least 2 hours or up to 24 hours.

STEAMED PEEL-AND-EAT SHRIMP
WITH **OLD BAY SEASONING**

SERVES 4

The recipe for this irresistible party food is an on-the-grill answer to the old French technique of cooking fish *en papillote*, or in a parchment-paper parcel. Here, shrimp are cooked in an aluminum foil packet over high heat, which steams them in beer, lime, and seasonings. Note that the timing will vary based on the size of the shrimp; get the biggest you can find for a dramatic impact at the table.

Be sure to add the beer, lime, cilantro, and Old Bay to the pan in the order indicated; adding the liquid first helps the Old Bay adhere to the shrimp.

I POUND JUMBO SHRIMP
(ABOUT 16 SHRIMP), UNPEELED

½ CUP LIGHT BEER (PREFERABLY
BUD LIGHT OR MILLER LITE)

I LIME, CUT INTO 6 TO 8 WEDGES

¼ CUP EXTRA VIRGIN OLIVE OIL

¼ CUP FRESH CILANTRO LEAVES

2 TABLESPOONS OLD BAY SEASONING

TO DRINK
AROMATIC WHITE
AMBER BEER

Lay a large sheet of heavy-duty aluminum foil in a large cast-iron skillet, pressing it down and allowing the excess foil to fall over the sides. Arrange the shrimp on the foil in a single layer, or as close to a single layer as possible.

Pour the beer over the shrimp. Squeeze the juice from the lime wedges over the shrimp and scatter the wedges on top. Drizzle the shrimp with the oil and strew the cilantro leaves over them. Sprinkle with the Old Bay seasoning.

Lay another large sheet of foil over the skillet. Crimp the edges of the 2 sheets together to create a well-sealed packet. Remove the packet from the skillet, taking care to support it from the bottom and keep the liquid from leaking out.

Prepare your grill for grilling (see pages 96–100).

Set the packet on the grill over the hot spot and grill for 3 minutes. Remove the packet from the heat and let stand for 2 minutes. (You can also cook the packet in the skillet on the stovetop. Cook it over medium heat for 10 minutes after you hear the liquid inside begin to boil.) Slash the packet open with a knife and serve the shrimp directly from the packet.

TUNA TARTARE
WITH **SCALLION, LEMON,** AND **SOY**

SERVES 4 (MAKES I CUP TARTARE)

Because this recipe uses lemon zest rather than juice, it can be made a bit ahead of time—just enough to get it done before you cook dinner or before your first guests show up.

I TEASPOON WHITE SESAME SEEDS

8 OUNCES SUSHI-GRADE TUNA, VERY FINELY DICED

I TABLESPOON SOY SAUCE

I TEASPOON FINELY GRATED LEMON ZEST

I TEASPOON SESAME OIL

I TABLESPOON EXTRA VIRGIN OLIVE OIL

2 TEASPOONS FINELY CHOPPED FRESH CILANTRO LEAVES

I SCALLION, I TABLESPOON WHITE PORTION, MINCED, AND I TABLESPOON GREEN PORTION, THINLY SLICED

RICE CRACKERS, FOR SERVING

TO DRINK
BLOND BEER

Heat a large, heavy-bottomed sauté pan over medium-high heat. Add the sesame seeds and cook, shaking and stirring the seeds, until golden brown, 2 to 3 minutes. Transfer the seeds to a large glass bowl and let cool completely before proceeding.

Add the tuna, soy, lemon zest, sesame oil, extra virgin olive oil, cilantro, and white scallion to the bowl with the sesame seeds and stir until well incorporated. Cover and chill for 15 to 20 minutes, but no longer.

To serve, scatter the green scallion over the surface of the tartare. Fill a bowl, slightly larger than the bowl holding the tartare, halfway with chipped ice. Set the bowl of tartare into the bowl of ice with a spoon and pass the crackers alongside in another bowl, letting everyone spread tartare onto rice crackers.

SMOKED SALMON AND EGG SALAD
ON **TOASTED SOURDOUGH BREAD**

SERVES 6 TO 8 (MAKES 40 PIECES)

Smoked salmon and hard-boiled eggs get along great together. Here, store-bought salmon (splurge on your favorite brand, or the best you can find) is tossed with crème fraîche, dill, onion, and lemon. That mixture is swiped on small toasts and topped with a spoonful of egg salad. The egg salad isn't the gloppy variety dripping with mayonnaise that you might remember from your grade-school lunch box. There's just enough mayonnaise to bind the other ingredients together, so the flavor and texture of the egg dominates. Try to get your hands on a good sourdough for this; it has the perfect flavor and durable texture for these toppings.

This recipe also shares my trick for just-toasted-enough bread for croutons, hors d'oeuvres, and sandwiches: keep a squeeze bottle of olive oil on hand. Drizzle the bread with oil, arrange the slices on a baking sheet, and pass them under a preheated broiler just long enough to slightly brown them.

The salmon salad and egg salad recipes are separated out on their own here so you can call on them for sandwiches and other uses.

TEN ¼-INCH-THICK SLICES SOURDOUGH BREAD, QUARTERED

¼ CUP EXTRA VIRGIN OLIVE OIL

KOSHER SALT

SMOKED SALMON SALAD (RECIPE FOLLOWS)

EGG SALAD (RECIPE FOLLOWS)

4 FRESH DILL SPRIGS, SEPARATED INTO SMALL PIECES

Preheat the broiler.

Arrange the sourdough bread pieces on a baking sheet. Drizzle with the extra virgin olive oil and sprinkle with salt to taste. Broil until lightly golden and crisp on the outside but still soft, 1 to 2 minutes.

Spread some smoked salmon salad on each piece of bread. Spoon some egg salad on top.

To serve, arrange the toasts on a serving platter and garnish with the dill.

SMOKED SALMON SALAD

MAKES 1¾ CUPS

8 OUNCES SMOKED SALMON, FINELY DICED (ABOUT 1 CUP DICED)

¼ CUP PLUS 1 TABLESPOON CRÈME FRAÎCHE OR SOUR CREAM

¼ CUP FINELY DICED CELERY

¼ CUP FINELY DICED RED ONION

2 TEASPOONS GRATED LEMON ZEST

1 TABLESPOON FRESHLY SQUEEZED LEMON JUICE

1 TABLESPOON MINCED FRESH DILL FRONDS

FRESHLY GROUND BLACK PEPPER

KOSHER SALT

Put the salmon, the ¼ cup crème fraîche, the celery, onion, lemon zest and juice, dill, and ¼ teaspoon pepper in a bowl. Toss and refrigerate until cold, at least 30 minutes.

BREAK POINT
The salmon can be covered and refrigerated for up to 6 hours.

When ready to proceed, stir in the remaining 1 tablespoon crème fraîche and season to taste with salt.

EGG SALAD

MAKES ¾ CUP

½ TEASPOON CELERY SEEDS

2 HARD-BOILED EGGS, MINCED

3 TABLESPOONS MAYONNAISE

1 TEASPOON GRATED LEMON ZEST

½ TEASPOON FRESHLY GROUND BLACK PEPPER

KOSHER SALT

TO DRINK
CRISP/FRESH WHITE

Heat a sauté pan over medium-high heat and add the celery seeds. Toast, shaking and stirring, until fragrant, 1 to 2 minutes. Transfer the seeds to a small bowl and let cool completely.

Add the remaining ingredients, except the salt, to the bowl with the celery seeds. Season to taste with salt and stir until well integrated.

BREAK POINT
The egg salad can be covered and refrigerated for up to 6 hours.

LEMON-MARINATED SHRIMP
AND **BRUSCHETTA-STYLE TOMATOES**

SERVES 4 TO 6

Here's a crowd-pleasing, warm version of shrimp cocktail. The shrimp are marinated in lemon, cilantro, sweet Spanish paprika, and other spices before being grilled. The cocktail sauce is replaced by bruschetta-style tomatoes, based on those served on the popular Italian starter. Peeled and finely diced, then tossed with basil, they're a fresh way to offset the shrimp and the char flavor of the grill.

Attention to a few details will really put this over the top: be sure that you mash the garlic that goes into both the shrimp marinade and the tomato mixture; turning it to a pasty consistency is crucial to getting both components tasting right. Select a good extra virgin olive oil in the bruschetta-style tomatoes to bring out their flavor. Finally, be sure to crack rather than grind the black pepper. Cracked pepper is more elusive and has more impact than ground; you don't get it in every bite, but when you find it, you know it.

1½ TEASPOONS GROUND CORIANDER

I TEASPOON GROUND CUMIN

¼ CUP GRATED LEMON ZEST

¼ CUP PLUS 2 TABLESPOONS FRESHLY SQUEEZED LEMON JUICE

3 TABLESPOONS MINCED FRESH CILANTRO LEAVES

I TABLESPOON SWEET SPANISH PAPRIKA

I TABLESPOON PULVERIZED GARLIC (SEE PAGE 21)

1½ TEASPOONS CAYENNE PEPPER

KOSHER SALT

2 POUNDS JUMBO SHRIMP (ABOUT 24 SHRIMP), PEELED

BRUSCHETTA-STYLE TOMATOES (RECIPE FOLLOWS)

Toast the coriander and cumin in a dry skillet over high heat until the spices smell pungent, about 30 seconds. Transfer to a bowl and let cool completely.

Add the lemon zest and juice, cilantro, paprika, garlic, cayenne, and 1½ teaspoons salt to the bowl and mix well. Add the shrimp and toss in the mixture. Cover and refrigerate for 2 hours.

BREAK POINT
The shrimp can be refrigerated for up to 6 hours.

Prepare your grill for grilling or preheat a cast-iron pan (see pages 96–100).

Remove the shrimp from the marinade and shake off any excess marinade. Grill over high heat for 2½ minutes, then turn the shrimp over and grill until firm and pink, approximately 2½ minutes more.

Put the tomatoes in the well of a serving platter. Arrange the grilled shrimp on top and serve.

BRUSCHETTA-STYLE TOMATOES

MAKES 1½ CUPS

6 PLUM TOMATOES, PEELED (SEE PAGE 40), CORED, SEEDED, AND FINELY DICED

3 TABLESPOONS EXTRA VIRGIN OLIVE OIL

6 GARLIC CLOVES, PULVERIZED (SEE PAGE 21)

I TABLESPOON BALSAMIC VINEGAR

I TEASPOON FINELY CHOPPED FRESH BASIL (ABOUT 4 LEAVES)

½ TEASPOON KOSHER SALT

½ TEASPOON CRACKED BLACK PEPPER

TO DRINK
BLOND OR AMBER BEER

Mix all the ingredients in a bowl, cover, and refrigerate for 2 hours or up to 24 hours.

WARM CRABMEAT TARTLETS
WITH **SPICY DIJON CREAM**

SERVES 8 (MAKES 24 TARTLETS)

I throw just about every crab-friendly ingredient into these little tartlets: onions, garlic, corn, cream, and jalapeños for heat. A great summer starter, these can also be made in other seasons with defrosted frozen corn.

2 TABLESPOONS CORN OIL OR OTHER NEUTRAL OIL SUCH AS GRAPESEED OR CANOLA

½ CUP VERY FINELY DICED WHITE ONIONS

2 TEASPOONS FINELY MINCED GARLIC

¼ CUP FRESH CORN KERNELS (SCRAPED FROM I COB), ROUGHLY CHOPPED

½ TEASPOON GROUND CORIANDER

2 TEASPOONS SEEDED, MINCED JALAPEÑO

¾ CUP HEAVY CREAM

2 TABLESPOONS DIJON MUSTARD

½ POUND LUMP CRABMEAT, PICKED FREE OF SHELL FRAGMENTS

2 TEASPOONS MINCED FRESH BASIL LEAVES

2 TEASPOONS GRATED LEMON ZEST

I TABLESPOON MINCED FRESH FLAT-LEAF PARSLEY LEAVES

KOSHER SALT

FRESHLY GROUND BLACK PEPPER

I LARGE EGG

I POUND STORE-BOUGHT PUFF PASTRY, THAWED

TO DRINK
OAKY/FULL-BODIED WHITE
FIZZY/SPARKLING WINE

Heat the oil in a heavy-bottomed, stainless-steel sauté pan over medium-high heat. Add the onions, garlic, and corn and cook until softened but not browned, approximately 4 minutes. Stir in the coriander and jalapeño and cook for 1 minute. Add the cream and mustard, bring to a boil, and continue to boil until the cream is reduced by one-third, 4 to 5 minutes.

Add the crabmeat, stir well to incorporate, and remove the pan from the heat. Stir in the basil, lemon zest, parsley, 1 tablespoon salt, and ¼ teaspoon pepper. Set aside and let cool to room temperature.

Put half of the crab mixture in a food processor fitted with the steel blade. Add the egg and pulse to break down and integrate the mixture, but do not totally break down or liquefy it. Fold the pureed mixture back into the rest of the original mixture.

BREAK POINT
The mixture can be covered and refrigerated for up to 24 hours.

Preheat the oven to 400°F.

Unroll the thawed puff pastry and cut it into 24 squares. Push 1 square down into each well of a tartlet or mini-muffin tin (1½ inches or 1¾ inches in diameter each). Pierce the bottom of each shell or cup 5 or 6 times with a fork and bake the shells for 5 minutes.

Add 1 tablespoon of the crab mixture to each tartlet shell and bake until lightly golden brown on top, approximately 10 minutes.

(CONTINUED)

If baking ahead of time, bake for 7 minutes, let cool, then cover and refrigerate until ready to serve. Re-warm for 3 to 4 minutes in an oven preheated to 350°F.

Arrange the tartlets on a serving plate or platter and serve immediately.

CHICKEN LIVER MOUSSE,
CRISP SHALLOTS, BRIOCHE, AND PORT REDUCTION

SERVES 4 TO 6

Chicken liver can do a pretty good impression of foie gras if you do enough to ratchet up its flavor. Here, chicken livers are cooked in butter, the pan is deglazed with port and cognac, and the mixture is enriched with cream. It's then pureed and pushed through a strainer to make it silky smooth. After a night of refrigeration, it's spread on brioche, then topped with crispy shallots and fresh parsley.

4 TABLESPOONS (½ STICK) UNSALTED BUTTER

¾ CUP FINELY DICED WHITE ONIONS

8 OUNCES FRESH CHICKEN LIVERS, TRIMMED

KOSHER SALT

¼ TEASPOON FRESHLY GROUND BLACK PEPPER

¼ CUP PLUS I TABLESPOON RED PORT

3 TABLESPOONS COGNAC

¼ TEASPOON GROUND ALLSPICE

½ TEASPOON FINELY GRATED LEMON ZEST

¼ TEASPOON CHOPPED FRESH THYME LEAVES

I TABLESPOON HEAVY CREAM

8 SLICES BRIOCHE, TOASTED UNTIL CRISP, QUARTERED

CRISP SHALLOTS (RECIPE FOLLOWS)

LEAVES FROM I BUNCH FRESH FLAT-LEAF PARSLEY

COARSE SEA SALT

TO DRINK
LIGHT/FRUIT-FORWARD RED

Melt 2 tablespoons of the butter in a heavy-bottomed sauté pan over medium-high heat. Add the onions and sauté until lightly browned, approximately 7 minutes. Transfer to a food processor fitted with the steel blade.

Lay the chicken livers on paper towels and season with 1 teaspoon kosher salt and pepper. Melt the remaining 2 tablespoons butter in the sauté pan over high heat, add the livers, and cook until browned, 3 to 4 minutes. Transfer the livers to the food processor with the onions.

Deglaze the sauté pan with the port and cognac and add the allspice, lemon zest, thyme, and cream. Bring to a simmer, reduce by one-third, 2 to 3 minutes, and transfer to the food processor with the livers and onions. Puree until smooth.

Push the chicken liver puree through a coarse-mesh strainer. (If you don't have a coarse-mesh strainer, skip this step.) Transfer the mixture to a 6-ounce ramekin or small bowl, cover with plastic wrap, and refrigerate overnight.

BREAK POINT
The mousse can be refrigerated for up to 2 days.

To serve, spread the mousse on the brioche points and arrange on a platter. Garnish with the crisp shallots, parsley, and sea salt to taste. Or put each component out in its own bowl or plate and let everyone compose his or her own.

CRISP SHALLOTS

MAKES 3½ CUPS

In addition to this dish, these are delicious scattered over salads. This recipe makes a bit more than is really needed here; I highly recommend snacking on the extra.

2 TABLESPOONS ALL-PURPOSE FLOUR

½ CUP MILK

3 TABLESPOONS COARSE CORNMEAL

KOSHER SALT

FRESHLY GROUND BLACK PEPPER

CORN OIL OR OTHER NEUTRAL OIL SUCH AS GRAPESEED OR CANOLA, FOR FRYING

6 SHALLOTS, VERY THINLY SLICED AND SEPARATED INTO RINGS

Put the flour in a bowl and gradually whisk in the milk to form a smooth mixture. Whisk in the cornmeal, then the ½ teaspoon salt and ¼ teaspoon pepper.

Pour the oil into a deep-sided pan to a depth of 3 inches and heat to 375°F.

Dip the shallot rings in the batter, allowing any excess batter to run off. Fry the shallots in batches in the oil until crisp and golden brown, approximately 1 minute. Use tongs or a slotted spoon to transfer the shallots to a paper-towel-lined plate to drain and immediately season to taste with salt.

MOROCCAN-SPICED
LAMB CHOPS

MAKES 14 TO 16 LAMB CHOPS

If you love a flavorful char on red meat, try these lamb chops. A dry rub of high-impact spices is spread on two lamb racks. When grilled, the spices are essentially toasted right onto the meat, releasing their flavor and fusing them together. Then you separate the chops and serve them as eat-with-your-hands appetizers.

I TEASPOON GARLIC POWDER

½ TEASPOON CAYENNE PEPPER

¾ TEASPOON GROUND CUMIN

I TEASPOON FRESHLY GROUND BLACK PEPPER

I TEASPOON GROUND FENNEL SEEDS

¼ TEASPOON DRIED SAGE

I TEASPOON DRY MUSTARD

I TEASPOON KOSHER SALT

¼ TEASPOON GROUND NUTMEG

¼ CUP CORN OIL OR OTHER NEUTRAL OIL SUCH AS GRAPESEED OR CANOLA

2 BABY LAMB RACKS, 7 OR 8 BONES EACH, BONES CLEANED, ⅛ INCH FAT LEFT ON EXTERIOR OF 1¼-INCH-DIAMETER LOIN

TO DRINK
SPICY RED
RICH/DARK BEER

Put all the ingredients except the lamb in a bowl and stir together. Rub the mixture all over the lamb. Set aside to marinate for 1 hour.

Prepare a grill for grilling or preheat a cast-iron pan (see pages 96–100).

Wrap the bones of the lamb racks with aluminum foil and grill over medium-high heat for 6 to 7 minutes on either side, or until the internal temperature on an instant-read thermometer reaches 110° to 115°F. Transfer to a clean, dry surface and let rest for 10 minutes.

To serve, slice the lamb into chops at each bone, arrange on a platter, and serve.

SALADS AND SMALL PLATES

Flexible Fare for Starters or Light Lunches

In the introduction, I mentioned that my New American steakhouse cooking updates rather than discards the classics. That is especially true in this chapter, which looks to dishes like tomato and onion salad, chopped salad, and crab cakes for inspiration.

My philosophy of starters and salads also tracks the traditional steakhouse one pretty closely: I like to stimulate the palate without killing the appetite. So there are a lot of dishes in this chapter that are, bottom line, light. But they're packed with big flavors, like the tomato salad with herbs, lobster salad with mango dressing, and grilled steak salad with peanut-lime sauce.

Of course, great ingredients are always important, but the vegetables in these recipes are so front and center that getting the best possible ones is especially crucial. Taken-for-granted ingredients like tomatoes, onions, watercress, and lettuce all play major roles in these dishes, so going out of your way to hit an organic grocery or farmers' market will pay especially big dividends.

SLICED BEEFSTEAK TOMATOES AND SWEET ONIONS

WITH **FRESH HERBS** AND **BLUE CHEESE CROUTONS**

SERVES 4

This understated salad has lots of peaks and valleys of flavor, some more subtle than others. Rather than mincing them together, you let each of the herbs—basil, dill, chives, parsley, and mint—show up in whole leaves or large pieces, so each bite's a little different from any other. That, considering that the tomatoes, blue cheese, and unexpectedly sweet onions provide plenty of contrasting tastes and textures, is all you need to make this a winner.

For the best results, prepare the salad at the height of tomato season in late summer, and don't overdress it. If your market doesn't sell sweet onions, soak white or Spanish onion slices in ice water for 10 to 15 minutes to soften their flavor.

3 RED BEEFSTEAK TOMATOES, CUT INTO ½-INCH SLICES

2 YELLOW BEEFSTEAK TOMATOES, CORED AND EACH CUT INTO 6 WEDGES

2 VIDALIA, WALLA WALLA, OR OTHER SWEET ONIONS, CUT INTO ¼-INCH-THICK SLICES, INNER RINGS SEPARATED

8 FRESH BASIL LEAVES, STACKED, ROLLED, AND THINLY SLICED CROSSWISE

6 FRESH DILL SPRIGS, LEAVES SEPARATED

6 FRESH CHIVES, CUT INTO 2-INCH LENGTHS

LEAVES FROM 4 FRESH FLAT-LEAF PARSLEY SPRIGS, THINLY SLICED

LEAVES FROM 4 FRESH MINT SPRIGS, THICKLY SLICED

12 CHERRY TOMATOES, HALVED

KOSHER SALT

COARSELY GROUND BLACK PEPPER

2 TABLESPOONS EXTRA VIRGIN OLIVE OIL

BLUE CHEESE CROUTONS (RECIPE FOLLOWS)

To make 4 salads, use about a quarter of each ingredient in each salad. You can make the salads one at a time, or line up 4 plates assembly-line fashion and make them all at once.

Arrange the red tomato slices in an overlapping circle in the center of a serving plate. Put the yellow beefsteak wedges on top of the red tomato slices.

Stack the onion rings on top of the tomatoes. Garnish the salad with the basil, dill, chives, parsley, and mint, scattering them around to establish different flavors throughout the salad.

Decoratively arrange the cherry tomatoes around the perimeter of the plate. Season the salad with 1 tablespoon salt and 1 teaspoon pepper, and drizzle extra virgin olive oil over the top. Serve with the croutons alongside.

BLUE CHEESE CROUTONS

MAKES 6 CROUTONS

4 OUNCES BLUE CHEESE, IDEALLY
STILTON OR FOURME D'AMBERT,
SOFTENED AT ROOM TEMPERATURE

THREE $\frac{1}{2}$-INCH-THICK SLICES
SOURDOUGH BREAD, HALVED
(OR 6 DIAGONAL SLICES BAGUETTE
OR FICELLE)

I TABLESPOON PLUS I$\frac{1}{2}$ TEASPOONS
EXTRA VIRGIN OLIVE OIL

TO DRINK
LIGHT/FLORAL WHITE
AMBER BEER

Preheat the oven to 350°F.

Put the softened cheese in a bowl and beat with a wooden spoon until creamy.

Brush the bread with the oil and arrange the slices in a single layer on a baking sheet. Bake in the oven until golden brown and lightly crisped, 3 to 4 minutes. Remove the sheet from the oven and remove the bread from the sheet. Spread some of the blue cheese on each crouton.

BREAK POINT
The croutons can be prepared up to 1 hour in advance and kept, covered loosely with plastic wrap, at room temperature.

MIXED GREENS SALAD,
CRISP PARMESAN CUPS, AND SHERRY VINAIGRETTE

SERVES 4

I generally favor simple presentations at home, but sometimes a cool presentation can really put a dish over the top. If something impressive can come together easily, then why not? This recipe shows you how to make a little serving cup from Parmesan cheese, which is easier than it sounds. It's a classic "impress your friends" kind of dish that makes a very simple salad seem special. If you don't own a microplane grater (see page 18), put coarsely grated cheese in a food processor fitted with the steel blade and pulse until the cheese looks like bread crumbs.

2 CUPS FINELY GRATED PARMIGIANO-REGGIANO CHEESE (ABOUT 8 OUNCES)

8 CUPS GENTLY CHOPPED MESCLUN GREENS

1/2 CUP FINELY DICED SHALLOTS

SHERRY VINAIGRETTE (PAGE II)

KOSHER SALT

FRESHLY GROUND BLACK PEPPER

2 RED BEEFSTEAK TOMATOES, CORED AND HALVED LENGTHWISE, CUT INTO 1/2-INCH SLICES

2 YELLOW BEEFSTEAK TOMATOES, CORED AND HALVED LENGTHWISE, CUT INTO 1/2-INCH SLICES

TO DRINK
OAKY/FULL-BODIED WHITE
LIGHT/FRUIT-FORWARD RED

Preheat the oven to 375°F.

On a nonstick or parchment-lined baking sheet, form the grated Parmigiano-Reggiano into 4 circles, 7 inches in diameter. Put 2 drinking glasses or tumblers with bases of approximately 3 inches upside down on a work space near the oven. (If you don't have drinking glasses with bases that wide, use the bottom of a can.)

Bake until the cheese melts and turns lightly golden, 6 to 8 minutes.

Remove the pan from the oven. Do the following quickly, while the cheese is still soft and pliable: Carefully lift each cheese circle from the sheet (a wide rubber spatula is a good tool for this) and drape it over the inverted glass to form a shallow cup. As it cools, the cheese will harden into a wavy shape that you can manipulate with your hands. Allow to cool and harden completely.

Put the greens and shallots in a large bowl. Dress with 3 to 4 table-spoons of the vinaigrette and season to taste with salt and pepper.

To serve, divide the dressed greens among the cheese cups. Arrange alternating slices of red and yellow tomatoes over the center of each of 4 serving plates. Set a filled cheese cup on top of the tomatoes in the center of each plate. Drizzle the tomatoes with the remaining vinaigrette and season to taste with salt and pepper. Serve at once.

CHOPPED VEGETABLE SALAD
WITH **SMOKED BACON** AND **RED WINE VINAIGRETTE**

SERVES 6 TO 8

My father used to make a super-tangy vinaigrette that we ate so much when I was a kid that I feel like it's become part of my DNA. I've borrowed it to dress this crisp and crunchy salad of haricots verts, cucumber, tomatoes, and onions. This is the only dressing that I shake in the bottle, just like Dad used to do.

This salad uses a lot of dressing. To keep everything crisp, don't dress it until the last second. If you have any vegetarians at the table, serve the smoked bacon on the side in a small bowl.

KOSHER SALT

1½ CUPS HARICOTS VERTS CUT INTO ¾-INCH PIECES (FROM ABOUT 6 OUNCES BEANS)

I POUND DOUBLE-SMOKED SLAB BACON, SKINNED AND CUT CROSSWISE INTO ¼- TO ½-INCH PIECES

3 CUPS FINELY CHOPPED MIXED BABY GREENS

6 CUPS FINELY CHOPPED HEARTS OF ROMAINE LETTUCE (FROM ABOUT 2 HEADS LETTUCE)

1½ CUPS PEELED, DICED CUCUMBER

2 CUPS CORED, DICED BEEFSTEAK TOMATOES (FROM ABOUT 3 MEDIUM TOMATOES)

1½ CUPS DICED RED ONIONS

RED WINE VINAIGRETTE (RECIPE FOLLOWS)

TO DRINK
SMOOTH/MEDIUM-BODIED RED

Bring a pot of lightly salted water to a boil. Fill a large bowl halfway with ice water. Add the beans to the boiling water and blanch them for 5 to 6 minutes. Use a slotted spoon to transfer them to the ice water to cool them and stop the cooking. Drain and set aside.

Put the bacon in a pot with 2 cups water. Bring to a boil over medium heat and let boil until the water evaporates, approximately 15 minutes. Let the bacon fry in the fat that remains in the pot until crisp, approximately 8 more minutes, stirring to keep it from scorching. Use tongs or a slotted spoon to transfer the bacon to a paper-towel-lined plate to drain.

To serve, put the bacon, haricots verts, greens, lettuce, cucumber, tomatoes, and onions in a bowl. Drizzle with the vinaigrette, toss well, divide among 6 to 8 plates, and serve at once.

Bonus Points
You can substitute other vegetables, such as asparagus, summer squash, and sweet peppers, for the ones in this salad. Trim and/or seed them, cut into ¾-inch pieces, and blanch each separately following the technique for blanching the haricots verts.

RED WINE VINAIGRETTE

MAKES 1¾ CUPS

1¼ CUPS EXTRA VIRGIN OLIVE OIL

½ CUP RED WINE VINEGAR

I TABLESPOON KOSHER SALT

I TABLESPOON GARLIC POWDER

½ TEASPOON FRESHLY GROUND
BLACK PEPPER

Put all of the ingredients in a jar or bottle. Close tightly and shake well. Serve at room temperature.

SMOKED SALMON SALAD

WITH **ICEBERG LETTUCE, RED ONION,** AND **LEMON VINAIGRETTE**

SERVES 4

As most New Yorkers know, smoked salmon, cream cheese, and red onion are a sublime combination, especially on a freshly toasted bagel. Here, the trio becomes the basis of a salad, where it's rounded out with radishes, dill pickle, and—most important—lemon, in both lemon zest and one of my favorite dressings, lemon vinaigrette. If you want to more closely approximate the bagel experience, serve this with toast points.

½ CUP CREAM CHEESE (ABOUT 4 OUNCES), SOFTENED AT ROOM TEMPERATURE

I TEASPOON GRATED LEMON ZEST

KOSHER SALT

FRESHLY GROUND BLACK PEPPER

2½ CUPS JULIENNED ICEBERG LETTUCE (FROM ABOUT ½ HEAD LETTUCE)

½ MEDIUM RED ONION, HALVED AND CUT INTO VERY THIN SLICES

¼ CUP COARSELY CHOPPED FRESH DILL FRONDS PLUS SEVERAL FRONDS FOR GARNISH

½ CUP THINLY JULIENNED RADISHES

½ CUP THINLY JULIENNED GARLIC DILL PICKLE, PREFERABLY FROM I LARGE PICKLE (LARGE PICKLES HAVE A BETTER PROPORTION OF FLESH TO SEEDS)

12 OUNCES SMOKED SALMON, THICKLY SLICED (12 TO 16 SLICES)

¼ CUP PLUS 2 TABLESPOONS LEMON VINAIGRETTE (PAGE II)

TO DRINK
FIZZY/SPARKLING WINE
BLOND BEER

Whip the cheese in a bowl with a whisk or wooden spoon until creamy and softened. Fold in the lemon zest and season to taste with salt and pepper.

BREAK POINT
The cheese can be prepared, covered, and refrigerated for up to 24 hours.

Toss the lettuce, onion, chopped dill, radishes, and pickle together in a bowl.

To serve, arrange 3 or 4 slices of salmon in an overlapping, fan pattern in the center of each of 4 chilled salad plates, letting the points of the salmon slices touch the perimeter of the dish's well.

Lightly dress the vegetable salad with ¼ cup of the vinaigrette. Mound a quarter of the mixture in the center of the plate, letting some salmon show around its circumference. Place a dollop (about 2 tablespoons) of whipped, seasoned cream cheese onto the exposed salmon and drizzle the salmon lightly with lemon vinaigrette. Garnish with dill fronds and serve.

Add ¼ ounce American sturgeon caviar to each portion, scattering it over the exposed salmon.

For a real treat, make this with homemade cured salmon:

DILL-VODKA-CURED SALMON

SERVES 4 TO 6

¼ CUP KOSHER SALT

¼ CUP SUGAR

I TEASPOON CRUSHED RED PEPPER FLAKES

¼ TEASPOON CRACKED CELERY SEEDS

¼ CUP CRACKED FENNEL SEEDS

I TABLESPOON FINELY GRATED LEMON ZEST

¼ CUP CHOPPED FRESH DILL FRONDS

1½ POUNDS SALMON FILLET, PREFERABLY WILD SALMON, SKIN ON, PREFERABLY FROM THE TAIL SECTION, ABOUT 1½ INCHES THICK (TRIM AND DISCARD THE NARROW 1½ INCHES FROM THE TAIL END TO HELP THE CASSEROLE REST EVENLY)

3 TABLESPOONS VODKA

Mix the salt, sugar, pepper flakes, celery seeds, fennel seeds, lemon zest, and dill in a small bowl. Use about 1 tablespoon of the mixture to coat the salmon skin, then place the salmon skin side down in an oval casserole dish large enough to hold it flat.

Evenly coat the rest of the salmon with the spices. Drizzle the salmon with the vodka.

Cover the casserole with plastic wrap and place a slightly smaller casserole on top to weight it down. Put a few 28- or 35-ounce tomato cans or other heavy cans on top of the second casserole dish, at each end, to evenly weight down the salmon. Place in the refrigerator with the weights and let cure for 48 hours.

You can keep the salmon, wrapped snugly in plastic, in the refrigerator for up to 4 days.

To serve, lift the salmon out of any liquid and gently scrape away the majority of the spices with the back of a knife. Slice the salmon thinly on the bias against the grain.

BAKED CRABMEAT GRATIN
WITH **BASIL** AND **JALAPEÑOS**

SERVES 10 TO 12

Bound with custard, this crab dish resembles a savory steamed pudding that may look richer than it actually is: there are lots of eggs and cream in the recipe, but the gratin serves ten to twelve people, so a little goes a long way.

  This is delicious with a simple salad of mesclun greens tossed with Lemon Vinaigrette (page 11).

¾ CUP WHITE ONIONS IN MEDIUM DICE

I POUND JUMBO LUMP CRABMEAT, PICKED FREE OF SHELL FRAGMENTS

6 JALAPEÑOS, ROASTED, PEELED, SEEDED, AND CUT INTO SMALL DICE (SEE PAGE 177)

¾ CUP DEFROSTED FROZEN CORN KERNELS

2 CUPS CORN BREAD IN ¾-INCH CUBES (USE STORE-BOUGHT OR THE RECIPE THAT FOLLOWS)

¼ CUP CHOPPED FRESH BASIL LEAVES

I TEASPOON MINCED FRESH THYME LEAVES

2 TEASPOONS GROUND CORIANDER

UNSALTED BUTTER, FOR GREASING THE BAKING DISH

2 CUPS HEAVY CREAM

7 LARGE EGG YOLKS

KOSHER SALT

FRESHLY GROUND BLACK PEPPER

⅔ CUP PANKO (JAPANESE) BREAD CRUMBS OR HOMEMADE UNSEASONED DRIED BREAD CRUMBS

Preheat the oven to 350°F.

Bring a pot of salted water to a boil over high heat. Add the onions to the pot and blanch for 20 seconds. Drain and set aside.

Gently stir together the onions, crabmeat, jalapeños, corn, corn bread, basil, thyme, and coriander in a bowl.

Butter an 8 by 12-inch ovenproof baking dish. Pour the mixture into the dish and spread it out evenly.

Put the cream and yolks in a bowl and mix well. Season with 1 tablespoon salt and 1 teaspoon pepper and pour this mixture over the crab mixture. Shake the dish gently to help the cream find its way to the bottom of the dish.

Wrap the dish with aluminum foil and set in a roasting pan. Fill the pan with warm water halfway up the sides of the baking dish. Bake until set (a toothpick inserted in the center comes out clean), approximately 40 minutes.

Remove the pan from the oven and preheat the broiler.

Top the crab mixture with the bread crumbs and cook under the broiler until the crumbs are golden, 2 to 3 minutes.

Cut into 3-inch squares and serve on warm salad plates.

CORN BREAD

I CUP FINE-GROUND CORNMEAL

$\frac{1}{4}$ CUP ALL-PURPOSE FLOUR

$\frac{1}{4}$ CUP SUGAR

I TABLESPOON BAKING POWDER

I TEASPOON BAKING SODA

KOSHER SALT

I$\frac{1}{4}$ CUPS MILK

I LARGE EGG

$\frac{1}{4}$ CUP UNSALTED BUTTER, MELTED
AND COOLED TO ROOM TEMPERATURE,
PLUS MORE FOR GREASING THE BAKING
DISH

TO DRINK
CRISP/FRESH WHITE
OAKY/FULL-BODIED WHITE

Put the cornmeal, flour, sugar, baking powder, baking soda, and 2 teaspoons salt in a bowl and mix together well. Put the milk, egg, and melted butter in a separate bowl and whip well to blend.

Add the wet ingredients to the dry ingredients and mix well with a wire whip until smooth. Let sit for 15 minutes.

Preheat the oven to 325°F.

Butter an 8-inch round baking dish and pour the batter into the dish. Bake until a toothpick inserted in the center comes out clean, 20 to 25 minutes. Remove from the oven and let cool for 20 minutes before slicing.

STEAMED LITTLENECK CLAMS,
ROASTED TOMATO BROTH,
AND GRILLED SOURDOUGH BREAD

SERVES 4

I've always believed that one of the best parts of eating clams is dunking hunks of bread into the broth. So I created a powerfully flavored broth for that very purpose. Of course, it also makes the clams delicious, but dipping that bread into the bowl is still one of my favorite indulgences.

12 PLUM TOMATOES, CORED AND SPLIT LENGTHWISE

3/4 CUP PLUS 2 TABLESPOONS EXTRA VIRGIN OLIVE OIL, PLUS MORE FOR DRIZZLING BREAD

5 FRESH THYME SPRIGS PLUS 2 TEASPOONS CHOPPED FRESH THYME LEAVES

1/4 CUP THINLY SLICED GARLIC (FROM 5 OR 6 LARGE CLOVES)

KOSHER SALT

FRESHLY GROUND BLACK PEPPER

1/2 CUP DRY WHITE WINE

2 1/2 POUNDS LITTLENECK CLAMS (ABOUT 24 CLAMS), CLEANED AND RINSED

2 TEASPOONS GRATED LEMON ZEST

1 LOAF SOURDOUGH BREAD, CUT INTO 1-INCH-THICK SLICES

1 TABLESPOON COLD UNSALTED BUTTER

TO DRINK
LIGHT/FLORAL WHITE
AMBER BEER

Preheat the oven to 325°F.

Lay the tomato halves on a baking sheet, cut side up. Drizzle with 1/4 cup of the olive oil and scatter the thyme sprigs, 2 tablespoons of the sliced garlic, 1 1/2 teaspoons salt, and 1 teaspoon pepper over the tomatoes. Drizzle 1/4 cup water onto the baking sheet around the tomatoes, which will help keep them moist while roasting. Roast the tomatoes until slightly browned and dry, 25 to 30 minutes.

Remove the sheet from the oven and transfer everything to a bowl. Add 1 cup water and 1/2 cup extra virgin olive oil. Cover and let steep for 30 minutes. Strain through a fine-mesh strainer set over a bowl, pressing down on the solids to extract as much flavorful liquid as possible. You should have about 1 3/4 cups tomato broth. Discard the solids and reserve the broth.

BREAK POINT
The broth can be covered and refrigerated for up to 72 hours.

Preheat the broiler.

Heat a large sauté pan over medium-high heat on the stove. Add the remaining 2 tablespoons oil and when hot, sauté the remaining 2 tablespoons garlic until browned, 1 to 2 minutes. Remove from the heat and add the white wine. Place the pan back on the stovetop and add the clams, lemon zest, thyme leaves, tomato broth, 2 teaspoons salt, and 1 teaspoon pepper. Cover and steam over high heat until the clams open, 5 to 6 minutes.

Meanwhile, arrange the bread on a baking sheet in a single layer. Drizzle with extra virgin olive oil and place under the broiler until just beginning to turn golden and crisp, 1 to 2 minutes per side. Remove from the oven and set aside.

Remove the cover from the sauté pan and discard any clams that have not opened. Gently stir in the butter.

To serve, divide the clams and broth among 4 wide, deep bowls and serve the bread alongside. Make sure to have an empty bowl or two handy for empty shells.

BONUS POINTS

For a more communal experience, serve the clams and broth from a giant bowl and let everyone serve themselves.

JUMBO LUMP CRAB CAKES
WITH MINCED VEGETABLE TARTAR SAUCE

MAKES 6 TO 8 CRAB CAKES

With the exception of some egg and the diced brioche added for binding and texture, these cakes are all crab, so buy the biggest, most voluptuous lumps of crabmeat you can find.

These are wonderful with Curried Peas and Corn (page 148) or a small serving of baby lettuces tossed with Lemon Vinaigrette (page 11).

½ CUP BRIOCHE OR WHITE BREAD IN ½-INCH DICE

I TABLESPOON DRY WHITE WINE

I LARGE EGG

¼ CUP MAYONNAISE

½ TEASPOON GRATED LEMON ZEST

2 TEASPOONS OLD BAY SEASONING

¼ TEASPOON DRY MUSTARD

½ TEASPOON TABASCO SAUCE

I TABLESPOON DIJON MUSTARD

½ TEASPOON WORCESTERSHIRE SAUCE

8 OUNCES JUMBO LUMP CRABMEAT, PICKED FREE OF SHELL FRAGMENTS

¼ CUP CORN OIL OR OTHER NEUTRAL OIL SUCH AS GRAPESEED OR CANOLA

MINCED VEGETABLE TARTAR SAUCE (PAGE 174), OPTIONAL

TO DRINK
OAKY/FULL-BODIED WHITE
AMBER BEER

Mix the bread and wine thoroughly in a bowl with a spoon. Let stand for 20 minutes.

Break the egg into a glass bowl and whip it with a fork. Use a spoon to remove and discard about half the egg. Add the mayonnaise, lemon zest, Old Bay, dry mustard, Tabasco, Dijon mustard, and Worcestershire. Mix well. Add the crabmeat and fold gently into the base. Add the bread and continue folding until half of the crabmeat falls apart into strands and the base comes together into a homogeneous mixture. Cover with plastic wrap and let stand in the refrigerator for 1 hour to set.

Form the mixture into 6 or 8 patties, approximately 2½ inches in diameter and 1 inch thick.

Heat the oil in a nonstick pan set over medium-high heat. When hot, fry the crab cakes until golden brown, about 4 minutes on each side. Reheat if necessary in a 350°F oven for 6 to 7 minutes.

To serve, place 1 crab cake on each of 6 to 8 warm salad plates, along with any desired accompaniments such as the Minced Vegetable Tartar Sauce or garnish.

Vegetable Roll with Ginger-Chile Sauce (page 37) and a Strip House Summertime Cooler (page 30)

Whipped Garlic Goat Cheese and Sherried Tomatoes on Cheese Crisps (page 39)

Steamed Peel-and-Eat Shrimp (page 45)

Moroccan-Spiced Lamb Chops (page 55)

Sliced Beefsteak Tomatoes and Sweet Onions with Fresh Herbs and Blue-Cheese Croutons (page 59)

Steamed Littleneck Clams, Roasted Tomato Broth, and Grilled Sourdough Bread (page 68)

Asparagus Soup with Blue Crab Claw (page 80)

Lemon-Pepper Marinated Chicken with Grilled Asparagus (page 108) and
Tabbouleh Salad with Lemon and Cucumber (page 147)

CHILLED LOBSTER COCKTAIL
WITH **MANGO-CUMIN CREAM** AND **WATERCRESS SALAD**

SERVES 4

Sweet, sensuous lobster, gently cooked in a simple court bouillon and paired with crunchy cucumber, acidic red onion, and an exotic mango-cumin cream, all on a bed of peppery watercress. What more do you need to know? This is a perfect starter for any occasion, from a backyard barbecue to a New Year's Eve dinner party.

8 BAY LEAVES

2 LEMONS, CUT INTO ¼-INCH-THICK SLICES

2 TABLESPOONS WHOLE BLACK PEPPERCORNS

½ CUP WHITE WINE VINEGAR

2 MAINE LOBSTERS, 1¼ POUNDS EACH, CLAWS INTACT

¼ CUP VERY THINLY JULIENNED PEELED CUCUMBER

⅛ CUP VERY THINLY SLICED RED ONION, RINGS SEPARATED

MANGO-CUMIN CREAM (PAGE 177)

I CUP WATERCRESS LEAVES WITH SOME STEM ATTACHED

8 FRESH CHIVES, CUT INTO 5-INCH LENGTHS

TO DRINK
AROMATIC WHITE
FIZZY / SPARKLING WINE
BLOND BEER

Pour 1 gallon water into a large soup pot or stockpot. Add the bay leaves, lemon slices, peppercorns, and vinegar. Bring to a boil over high heat. Fill a large bowl with ice water. With a large, sharp knife, kill the lobsters by inserting a knife right between their eyes and pulling it down like a lever. (This seems violent, but is actually the most humane way to kill them. If you prefer, you can add them alive to the boiling water.) When the water reaches a boil, add the lobsters and cook for 8 minutes.

Use tongs to transfer the lobsters to the ice water, submerging them and stopping the cooking as quickly as possible.

Separate the lobster tail and claws from each body. Use a mallet or the back of a heavy kitchen knife to crack the claws and "knuckles" of the lobster. Remove the meat. Lay the tail on a flat surface and cut lengthwise. Remove the tail meat and reserve. Cut the lobster tail into ½-inch chunks.

Dress the lobster tail chunks, knuckle meat, cucumber julienne, and sliced red onion in a bowl with 2 tablespoons of the mango-cumin cream.

To serve, put about a quarter of the watercress leaves in the bottom of each of 4 large martini glasses or parfait glasses. Spoon 2 tablespoons of the mango-cumin cream into each glass. Spoon in about a quarter of the dressed lobster meat and vegetables. Garnish each serving with some chopped chives, letting them stick up out of the parfait.

NEW YORK STRIP STEAK SALAD
WITH **JULIENNED VEGETABLES** AND **BLACK PEPPER DRESSING**

SERVES 6 TO 8 AS A STARTER OR 4 AS A SMALL MEAL

The highlight of this salad is the black pepper dressing, an emulsion that starts with an infused black pepper oil. By gently warming the oil and cracked black pepper, the flavor of the pepper mellows, losing most of its heat.

¼ CUP CORN OIL OR OTHER NEUTRAL OIL SUCH AS GRAPESEED OR CANOLA

2 NEW YORK STRIP STEAKS, CENTER CUT, ABOUT 1¾ INCHES THICK

KOSHER SALT

FRESHLY GROUND BLACK PEPPER

1 MEDIUM CARROT, JULIENNED

1 MEDIUM FENNEL BULB, TRIMMED AND JULIENNED

1 LARGE RED BELL PEPPER, JULIENNED

1 SMALL RED ONION, HALVED LENGTHWISE, THEN CORED AND CUT INTO PEGS (SEE PAGE 21)

1 CUP JULIENNED BUTTER LETTUCE OR ICEBERG LETTUCE LEAVES

1 TEASPOON GRATED LEMON ZEST

¼ CUP EXTRA VIRGIN OLIVE OIL

BLACK PEPPER DRESSING (RECIPE FOLLOWS)

TO DRINK
OAKY/FULL-BODIED WHITE
AMBER BEER

Preheat the oven to 475°F.

Pour the corn oil into a shallow pan or plate. Turn the steak in the oil to coat evenly and season with 2 tablespoons salt and 2 teaspoons pepper.

Heat a cast-iron pan over very high heat for about 5 minutes. Put the seasoned steaks in the pan and cook for 3 minutes on each side.

Put the pan in the oven and cook until the steaks reach an internal temperature of 110° to 115°F for medium rare, approximately 7 minutes. Remove the pan from the oven, remove the steaks from the pan, and allow them to rest for 6 to 7 minutes.

Put the carrot, fennel, bell pepper, red onion, butter lettuce, and lemon zest in a bowl and dress with the olive oil, ½ teaspoon salt, and ¼ teaspoon pepper.

To serve, arrange the salad on a large serving tray. Slice the steaks against the grain and arrange the slices on top of the salad. Pass the dressing in a small bowl on the side.

BLACK PEPPER DRESSING

MAKES 1½ CUPS

I CUP CORN OIL OR OTHER NEUTRAL OIL
SUCH AS GRAPESEED OR CANOLA

2 TEASPOONS CRACKED BLACK PEPPER

¼ CUP RED WINE VINEGAR

2 TABLESPOONS FRESHLY SQUEEZED
LEMON JUICE

I LARGE EGG YOLK

½ TEASPOON CHOPPED FRESH
THYME LEAVES

Warm the oil and pepper in a small pot for 5 to 6 minutes over medium heat. Remove the pot from the stove and let the oil cool to room temperature. (If you don't let the oil cool all the way down, the dressing won't emulsify properly.)

Whisk the vinegar and lemon juice together in a small bowl.

Put the egg yolk in a standing blender. Turn on the blender and add alternating quantities of the black pepper oil and vinegar-lemon mixture until all are incorporated. Transfer the dressing to a small bowl and stir in the thyme.

BREAK POINT
You can make the dressing up to 48 hours ahead of time. It tends to thicken, so thin it by whisking in a tablespoon or so of cold water.

BONUS POINTS
The black pepper oil is great drizzled over fish or shrimp.

GINGER-MARINATED
SKIRT STEAK SALAD
WITH CRISP NOODLES AND PEANUT-LIME DRESSING

SERVES 6

If you have the time, marinate the steak for the full twenty-four hours suggested. The acid in the marinade causes it to break down between the twelfth and twenty-fourth hour, resulting in a deeper penetration of flavor and a succulent result after grilling.

2 TABLESPOONS SESAME SEEDS, BLACK OR WHITE

I TABLESPOON MINCED GARLIC

2 TABLESPOONS PEELED, MINCED FRESH GINGER

¼ CUP PLUS 3 TABLESPOONS CHOPPED FRESH CILANTRO LEAVES

I TABLESPOON GRATED LIME ZEST

2 TEASPOONS GRATED ORANGE ZEST

I TABLESPOON SEEDED, MINCED JALAPEÑO

I TABLESPOON CRUSHED RED PEPPER FLAKES

⅓ CUP SOY SAUCE

4 POUNDS SKIRT STEAK, TRIMMED OF SILVER SKIN AND EXCESS FAT

CANOLA OIL, FOR FRYING

4 OUNCES ANGEL HAIR PASTA, COOKED AND DRAINED

KOSHER SALT

2 BUNCHES WATERCRESS, THICK STEMS DISCARDED

I MEDIUM FENNEL BULB, TRIMMED AND JULIENNED

I LARGE RED BELL PEPPER, JULIENNED

I SMALL RED ONION, HALVED LENGTHWISE, THEN CORED AND CUT INTO PEGS (SEE PAGE 2I)

I CUP JULIENNED BUTTER LETTUCE LEAVES

¼ CUP EXTRA VIRGIN OLIVE OIL

2 TABLESPOONS RED WINE VINEGAR

Toast the sesame seeds in a sauté pan over medium heat until lightly warmed and fragrant, approximately 3 minutes. Remove the pan from the heat.

Stir the garlic, ginger, the 3 tablespoons cilantro, the lime zest, orange zest, sesame seeds, jalapeño, pepper flakes, and soy sauce together in a large bowl. Add the steak, stir to coat with the marinade, cover, and refrigerate for 12 to 24 hours.

Prepare an outdoor grill for grilling (see pages 96–100). Remove the steak from the marinade and shake or wipe off any solids. Grill over high heat for 3 minutes on each side for rare to medium-rare. Remove the meat from the grill and let rest for 4 to 5 minutes before thinly slicing against the grain.

Or cook the steak under the broiler for the same amount of time. Check with an instant-read thermometer and remove the steak from the oven at 100°F; it will rise to about 115°F while resting.

Pour the canola oil into a deep-sided sauté pan to a depth of 1 inch. Heat the oil to 375°F. Deep-fry the pasta, in batches if necessary, until crisp and golden. Use a slotted spoon to transfer the pasta to a paper-towel-lined plate and season to taste with salt.

Mix the watercress, ¼ cup cilantro leaves, fennel, bell pepper, onion, lettuce leaves, and crisp pasta together in a bowl (the pasta should break up into smaller pieces).

Make a simple vinaigrette by whisking the olive oil, vinegar, ½ teaspoon salt, the garlic powder, and ⅛ teaspoon black pepper together in a bowl. Dress the salad with the vinaigrette.

½ TEASPOON GARLIC POWDER

FRESHLY GROUND BLACK PEPPER

PEANUT-LIME DRESSING
(RECIPE FOLLOWS)

¼ CUP CRACKED ROASTED PEANUTS

4 SCALLIONS, THINLY SLICED
DIAGONALLY

TO DRINK
LIGHT/FRUIT-FORWARD RED
RICH/DARK BEER

Divide the dressed salad among 6 serving plates and top with the sliced skirt steak. Drizzle each plate with peanut-lime dressing and top with roasted peanuts and sliced scallions.

PEANUT-LIME DRESSING

MAKES 1¼ CUPS

½ CUP DRY-ROASTED PEANUTS

¼ CUP PEANUT OIL

3 TABLESPOONS CREAMY
PEANUT BUTTER

3 TABLESPOONS FRESHLY SQUEEZED
LIME JUICE

KOSHER SALT

¼ TEASPOON SWEET SPANISH PAPRIKA

¼ TEASPOON CAYENNE PEPPER

3 TABLESPOONS CREAM OF COCONUT,
SUCH AS COCO LOPEZ

Process the peanuts and peanut oil in a food processor until smooth and grainy. Add the peanut butter, lime juice, 1 teaspoon salt, ¼ cup plus 3 tablespoons water, the paprika, cayenne, and cream of coconut and process until well mixed. If it seems too thick, add another tablespoon or so of water. Refrigerate for at least 4 hours before serving.

SOUPS

Bowl Them Over with These Seasonal Stunners

I love soups, especially when entertaining, because they're so convenient.

A lot of home cooks don't think much about making soup. Unless it's cold outside, causing us to crave certain ones, soups are just not on the radar of many home cooks. Maybe it's because so many of us grew up eating soup out of a can that it doesn't occur to us to make our own from scratch.

I strongly encourage you not to forget about soup when planning a meal. I especially like soups that take the palate on a wild ride. I try to jazz them up with other elements, making them texturally interesting, whether that means going a light and airy route or perhaps a more hearty and substantial one.

Throughout this chapter I call for a variety of strainers to attain the best possible texture. It's well worth the modest investment required to bulk up your collection of these devices to gain greater control over what you're cooking (see page 19).

The soups in this chapter are presented in a bowl, but keep other serving methods in mind. You can, for example, serve soup in coffee cups as a smaller starter, what we might call an *amuse* in a restaurant, or you can serve them in shot glasses as a smart and unexpected starter.

SPRING GARLIC SOUP

SERVES 8 TO 10

When you're looking for the pungent flavor of garlic without the halitosis, spring garlic just might be the answer to your prayers, especially when thickened with potato and mellowed with cream. Spring garlic is available only in May, when this soup is a great way to harness the season.

2 TABLESPOONS UNSALTED BUTTER

10 BULBS SPRING GARLIC, THINLY SLICED (IF MAKING AT OTHER TIMES OF YEAR, SUBSTITUTE 1½ CUPS GARLIC CLOVES, FROM 3 TO 4 LARGE HEADS; THINLY SLICE THE CLOVES)

1½ CUPS PEELED, DICED POTATO (FROM ABOUT 1 MEDIUM POTATO)

1 CUP DICED WHITE ONIONS

2 TEASPOONS CHOPPED FRESH THYME LEAVES

1 TEASPOON FINELY GRATED LEMON ZEST

½ CUP HEAVY CREAM

1 QUART VEGETABLE STOCK (PAGE 12) OR LOW-SODIUM, STORE-BOUGHT VEGETABLE BROTH

KOSHER SALT

FRESHLY GROUND BLACK PEPPER

TO DRINK
CRISP/FRESH WHITE

Melt the butter in a soup pot set over medium heat. Add the garlic, potato, and onions and cook until the butter is lightly browned, 5 to 6 minutes. Add the thyme, lemon zest, cream, stock, 1 tablespoon salt, and ½ teaspoon pepper and bring to a boil over high heat. Lower the heat and let simmer for 20 minutes, stirring occasionally.

BREAK POINT
If you leave out the cream, you can make the soup to this point; cool, cover, and refrigerate it for up to 3 days. Then gently reheat, add the cream, and proceed.

Use an immersion blender to blend the soup until uniformly smooth, or transfer to a standing blender and blend in batches until smooth. Divide among individual bowls and serve warm.

ASPARAGUS SOUP
WITH **BLUE CRAB CLAW**

SERVES 6

I love asparagus soup served warm so I can taste all the nuances of the vegetable. But it's important to distinguish warm from hot; when soup is hot, it can overwhelm the palate with heat rather than flavor. Here, the freshness of the asparagus is maintained by sautéing it off to the side, then blending it into the soup, transmitting its fresh flavor through the whole thing.

I find that blue crab claw has a great, largely unsung flavor, thanks to the fact that the working muscles in most animals, from land or sea, are often the most flavorful. Its character really comes alive in contrast to the green flavor of the asparagus and the silky texture of the soup.

¼ CUP PLUS 2 TABLESPOONS CORN OIL OR OTHER NEUTRAL OIL SUCH AS GRAPESEED OR CANOLA

3 POUNDS ANY SIZE ASPARAGUS, WASHED AND ROUGHLY CUT ON THE BIAS INTO 1-INCH SEGMENTS, TIPS RESERVED SEPARATELY

1 CUP ROUGHLY CUT WHITE ONIONS

1 TABLESPOON THINLY SLICED GARLIC

⅓ CUP PEELED POTATO IN ¼-INCH DICE

1 TEASPOON CRACKED CARAWAY SEEDS

¼ TEASPOON GROUND CUMIN

2 TEASPOONS CHOPPED FRESH THYME LEAVES

2 QUARTS VEGETABLE STOCK (PAGE 12) OR LOW-SODIUM, STORE-BOUGHT VEGETABLE BROTH, OR WATER

KOSHER SALT

FRESHLY GROUND BLACK PEPPER

1 TABLESPOON UNSALTED BUTTER

4 OUNCES BLUE CRAB CLAW MEAT

¼ TEASPOON GRATED LEMON ZEST

½ TEASPOON CHOPPED FRESH FLAT-LEAF PARSLEY LEAVES

Heat 1 tablespoon of the oil in a sauté pan over high heat. Add one-third of the asparagus and sauté until just cooked, but still bright green with no browning whatsoever, 2 to 3 minutes. Transfer the asparagus to a rimmed baking sheet, spreading the pieces out in a single layer so they cool as quickly as possible. Repeat with the remaining asparagus, adding 1 tablespoon oil before each batch, and gathering the sautéed batches on the sheet. Then heat 1 tablespoon oil in the pan, sauté the tips, and reserve them separately. Put the asparagus and tips in the refrigerator to finish cooling them and preserve their color and flavor.

Heat the remaining 2 tablespoons oil in a soup pot over medium-low heat. Add the onions, garlic, and potato and sauté until softened but not browned, 7 to 8 minutes. Add the caraway, cumin, and thyme and sauté until the spices and herbs are toasted and fragrant, 2 to 3 more minutes. Pour in the stock, raise the heat to high, and bring to a boil.

Season with 1 tablespoon salt and ½ teaspoon pepper, lower the heat, and let simmer for 25 minutes. Remove from the heat and let cool slightly.

BREAK POINT

You can prepare the soup's components to this point, then cool, cover, and refrigerate them separately.

Puree the cooked asparagus, except the tips, in a blender in small batches, then strain the soup through a fine-mesh strainer set over a bowl. Taste and adjust the seasoning, if necessary.

Return the soup to the pot and warm it over low heat while preparing the crab.

Melt the butter in a small sauté pan. Add the blue crab claw meat, lemon zest, and parsley and season to taste with salt. Warm the meat on the stove for 2 to 3 minutes over medium heat, gently tossing to coat it with the butter, zest, and parsley.

To serve, put a small mound of crab in the bottom of each of 6 soup plates. Top with some of the reserved asparagus tips. Pour the warmed asparagus soup around the crab and serve at once.

CHILLED YELLOW
TOMATO GAZPACHO

My gazpacho doesn't follow the original Spanish formula. There's no bread and no almonds; I use yellow rather than red tomatoes; and I add serrano chiles, which are three rungs up on the spice ladder above jalapeños. Also, the soup is blended until smooth. The oil in the marinade causes the soup to emulsify but you can still taste the distinct flavor of each vegetable, just as in the chunky, salsa-like original.

4 YELLOW BEEFSTEAK TOMATOES, CORED AND ROUGHLY CHOPPED

2 SMALL CUCUMBERS, PEELED AND ROUGHLY CHOPPED

1/4 CUP ROUGHLY CHOPPED WHITE ONION

2 TEASPOONS THINLY SLICED GARLIC

1/4 CUP ROUGHLY CHOPPED FRESH BASIL LEAVES

2 TABLESPOONS FRESH CILANTRO LEAVES

2 SCALLIONS, WHITE AND GREEN PARTS, ROUGHLY CHOPPED

1 1/2 CUPS EXTRA VIRGIN OLIVE OIL

1/2 CUP FRESHLY SQUEEZED LEMON JUICE

2 TABLESPOONS KOSHER SALT

1/2 TEASPOON FRESHLY GROUND BLACK PEPPER

1 SERRANO CHILE

TO DRINK
CRISP/FRESH WHITE
FIZZY/SPARKLING WINE
LIGHT-BODIED BEER

Toss all of the ingredients in a large bowl to mix well. Cover and let marinate in the refrigerator for at least 4 hours or up to 12 hours.

Blend the soup in batches in a blender until smooth. Return to the refrigerator and cool for at least 4 hours before serving chilled.

CORN SOUP

SERVES 8 TO 10

This soup is a puree made with onions and jalapeño to bring out the corn's sweetness. Check out the technique for making the soup with water and corncobs, which uses all parts of the corn to extract as much flavor as possible; it's more cost- and time-effective than using stock.

The avocado mousse is much more than just a garnish; it's like a guacamole without the texture. The avocado is pressed through a fine-mesh strainer to make it as smooth and creamy as possible, then punched up with ground cumin, lime juice, jalapeño, and cilantro.

$\frac{1}{4}$ CUP CORN OIL OR OTHER NEUTRAL OIL SUCH AS GRAPESEED OR CANOLA

1 CUP DICED WHITE ONIONS

1 JALAPEÑO, SEEDS INTACT, ROUGHLY CHOPPED, PLUS $\frac{1}{2}$ JALAPEÑO, SEEDED, ROUGHLY CHOPPED, AND SET ASIDE SEPARATELY

6 CUPS CORN KERNELS (FROM 6 TO 8 EARS CORN), COBS RESERVED

$2\frac{1}{4}$ TEASPOONS GROUND CUMIN

KOSHER SALT

FRESHLY GROUND BLACK PEPPER

$\frac{1}{4}$ CUP PLUS 2 TEASPOONS ROUGHLY CHOPPED FRESH CILANTRO LEAVES

$\frac{1}{2}$ CUP HEAVY CREAM

1 RIPE AVOCADO, PITTED AND ROUGHLY CHOPPED

2 TEASPOONS FRESHLY SQUEEZED LIME JUICE

TO DRINK
OAKY/FULL-BODIED WHITE

Heat the oil in a large, heavy-bottomed soup pot over medium-high heat. Add the onions, jalapeño with its seeds, and corn kernels and sauté over high heat until softened but not browned, 7 to 8 minutes. Add 2 teaspoons of the cumin, 1 tablespoon salt and 1 teaspoon pepper, and 2 quarts water and bring to a boil. Add the corncobs, lower the heat, and let simmer for 20 minutes.

Remove the pot from the heat and let the soup cool to room temperature. Use tongs to pick out and discard the cobs. Add the $\frac{1}{4}$ cup cilantro. Puree with an immersion blender or in a standing blender in batches.

For a more refined soup, strain the soup through a fine-mesh strainer to eliminate any fibrous bits of corn. Cover and chill the soup for at least 1 hour before serving.

BREAK POINT
The soup can be covered and refrigerated for up to 24 hours.

To make the avocado mousse, whip the heavy cream in a bowl until stiff and firm.

Pass the avocado through a fine-mesh sieve into a bowl. You should have just over $\frac{1}{2}$ cup of avocado puree.

(CONTINUED)

Grind the lime juice, remaining 2 teaspoons cilantro, seeded jalapeño, and remaining ¼ teaspoon cumin in a mortar and pestle to make a smooth paste. Fold the paste into the avocado, then fold in the cream. Season with ¼ teaspoon salt. Cover and chill for at least 1 hour before serving.

BREAK POINT
The mousse can be covered and refrigerated for up to 3 hours. Gently press a piece of plastic wrap on the surface of the mousse to keep any air from coming into contact with the avocado and prevent it from browning.

To serve, ladle about 1½ cups of soup into each bowl and top with a rounded spoonful of avocado mousse.

GREEN LENTIL SOUP
WITH **GRILLED COUNTRY HAM**

SERVES 8 TO 10

This is a sort of rustic version of split pea and ham soup made with firm French lentils (*lentilles du Puy*) and grilled country ham, with a touch of caraway added for a distinct bistro touch. This hearty soup can easily serve as a meal.

8 OUNCES COUNTRY HAM, CUT INTO ½-INCH-THICK SLICES

FRESHLY GROUND BLACK PEPPER

2 TABLESPOONS CORN OIL OR OTHER NEUTRAL OIL SUCH AS GRAPESEED OR CANOLA, PLUS MORE FOR BRUSHING THE HAM

1 CUP DICED WHITE ONIONS

¾ CUP DICED CELERY (FROM ABOUT 2 STALKS)

1 CUP DICED CARROT (FROM ABOUT 1 LARGE CARROT)

2 TEASPOONS PULVERIZED GARLIC (FROM 2 TO 3 CLOVES; SEE PAGE 21)

2 TEASPOONS GROUND CARAWAY SEEDS

1½ CUPS DRIED FRENCH GREEN LENTILS (LENTILLES DU PUY)

KOSHER SALT

1 BAY LEAF

2 TEASPOONS CHOPPED FRESH THYME LEAVES

⅛ TEASPOON CAYENNE PEPPER

8 TO 10 THICK SLICES SOURDOUGH BREAD (1 SLICE PER PERSON), LIGHTLY TOASTED

TO DRINK
SMOOTH/MEDIUM-BODIED RED

Preheat a grill or a cast-iron pan.

Lightly season the ham with pepper. Brush lightly with oil and grill until lightly browned, approximately 3 minutes per side. Transfer to a plate and let cool. When cool enough to handle, cut into strips and then use your fingers to shred each strip into ½-inch pieces.

Heat the 2 tablespoons oil in a large soup pot over high heat. Add the onions, celery, carrot, and garlic and sauté until softened but not browned, 4 to 5 minutes. Add the caraway and ham, reduce the heat to medium-high, and cook, stirring, for an additional 3 to 4 minutes. Add the lentils, 1 tablespoon salt, ¼ teaspoon pepper, the bay leaf, thyme, cayenne, and 10 cups water.

Bring to a boil, stirring occasionally. Reduce the heat and let simmer for 2½ hours. Stir more frequently during the final 20 to 30 minutes to break down the softened lentils.

Divide the soup among individual bowls and serve with 1 slice of bread per person.

BLACK BEAN SOUP

SERVES 6 TO 8

Black bean soup is easy to make because it doesn't take much to make the beans taste great; they absorb the flavor of anything they are cooked with. I puree my black bean soup so that all of the flavors come together in every bite. A last-second addition of lime juice sets off the spicy flavors with some welcome acidity.

I POUND BLACK BEANS, PICKED FREE OF PEBBLES AND OTHER IMPURITIES

¼ CUP VEGETABLE OIL

2 CUPS FINELY DICED WHITE ONIONS

3 TABLESPOONS MINCED GARLIC

1½ TEASPOONS GROUND CUMIN

I TEASPOON GROUND CORIANDER

5 CUPS CHICKEN STOCK (PAGE 13) OR LOW-SODIUM, STORE-BOUGHT CHICKEN BROTH

¼ CUP CHOPPED FRESH CILANTRO LEAVES

I TABLESPOON MINCED JALAPEÑO, WITH SEEDS

3 CUPS CANNED CRUSHED TOMATOES

2 TABLESPOONS ROUGHLY CHOPPED CANNED CHIPOTLE IN ADOBO

KOSHER SALT

2 BAY LEAVES

2 TABLESPOONS PLUS ½ TEASPOONS FRESHLY SQUEEZED LIME JUICE

TO DRINK
AMBER BEER

Put the black beans in a large pot with a lid and add 2 quarts cold water. Cover and allow to soak overnight, unrefrigerated. Or you can quick-soak the beans: Cover them in a heavy-bottomed pot with 3 inches of cold water and bring the water to a simmer. Cover the pot, turn off the heat, and let the beans soak until tender, 1 to 2 hours.

Heat the oil in a large, heavy-bottomed soup pot over high heat. Add the onions and garlic and sauté until softened but not browned, approximately 3 minutes. Add the cumin and coriander and toast, stirring, until fragrant, 1 to 2 minutes. Add the stock, cilantro, jalapeño, tomatoes, chipotle, 2 tablespoons salt, bay leaves, and 8 cups water and bring to a boil over high heat. Lower the heat and let simmer until the beans are softened, approximately 2 hours. Stir in the lime juice, taste, and season with more salt if necessary.

Puree the soup using an immersion blender, or in batches in a conventional standing blender.

BREAK POINT
Cool, cover, and refrigerate the soup for up to 3 days. Reheat gently, adding a few tablespoons water, if necessary, to loosen it up.

Ladle into individual bowls and serve.

BONUS POINTS
To serve black beans as a side dish, halve this recipe and skip the pureeing step.

LOBSTER BISQUE

SERVES 6

Lobster bisque is one of those dishes that make you realize why certain classics endure for generations. Its foundation of lobster, cognac, cream, tomato, and rice is just about perfect in its balance of flavors and textures. This recipe, from Strip House New York's chef de cuisine Rene Lenger, has a few original touches—like Arborio rice, usually reserved for risotto, and lemon zest, which takes these flavors to a whole new level.

4 BAY LEAVES

I LEMON, THINLY SLICED

I TABLESPOON BLACK PEPPERCORNS

1/4 CUP WHITE WINE VINEGAR

2 LOBSTERS, 1/4 POUNDS EACH

2 TEASPOONS CORIANDER SEEDS

2 TEASPOONS FENNEL SEEDS

1/4 BUNCH FRESH THYME

2 TABLESPOONS CORN OIL OR OTHER NEUTRAL OIL SUCH AS GRAPESEED OR CANOLA

1/4 CUP COGNAC

4 TABLESPOONS (1/2 STICK) UNSALTED BUTTER

I CARROT, ROUGHLY CHOPPED

2 CELERY STALKS, ROUGHLY CHOPPED

I FENNEL BULB, TRIMMED AND ROUGHLY CHOPPED

I MEDIUM ONION, ROUGHLY CHOPPED

3 TABLESPOONS TOMATO PASTE

3 1/2 CUPS HEAVY CREAM

1 1/2 CUPS MILK

2 TABLESPOONS ARBORIO RICE

1/4 BUNCH FRESH FLAT-LEAF PARSLEY

KOSHER SALT

FRESHLY GROUND BLACK PEPPER

2 TABLESPOONS SHERRY VINEGAR, OR TO TASTE

Pour 1 gallon water into a large, heavy-bottomed pot. Add the bay leaves, lemon slices, peppercorns, and vinegar and bring to a boil over high heat. As the water is coming to a boil, fill a large bowl halfway with ice water. Add the lobsters (see page 71) to the boiling liquid and cook for 8 minutes. Use tongs to transfer the lobsters to the ice water to stop the cooking.

Once cooled, separate the lobster tails and claws from the bodies. Crack the claws, remove the meat, and dice into 1/2-inch chunks. Lay each tail on a flat surface and cut it open lengthwise. Dice the meat into 1/2-inch chunks and set aside with the claw meat. Remove the tomalley and set it aside. Remove and discard the intestinal tract and stomach (the sac located behind the eyes). Do not discard the shells or lobster bodies. Using a heavy knife on a cutting board, cut the lobster shells and bodies into small pieces and set aside.

Toast the coriander seeds in a sauté pan over medium heat until fragrant, approximately 3 minutes. Transfer to a bowl to cool. Add the fennel seeds to the pan and toast until fragrant, approximately 3 minutes, then add to the bowl with the coriander. Once the seeds are cool, transfer them to a piece of cheesecloth. Add the thyme and tie the cheesecloth up into a bundle, called a bouquet garni.

(CONTINUED)

½ TEASPOON LEMON ZEST,
OR TO TASTE

TO DRINK
CRISP/FRESH WHITE
FIZZY/SPARKLING WINE

Heat the oil in a medium, heavy-bottomed saucepan over high heat. Add the lobster bodies, shells, and tomalley and pan-roast them until the shells are bright red, approximately 10 minutes. Remove the pan from the heat and, leaning away, carefully add the cognac. Let the alcohol burn off, approximately 2 minutes, stirring to loosen any flavorful bits stuck to the bottom of the pan.

Return the pan to the heat and add the butter, carrot, celery, chopped fennel, and onion. Cook until the vegetables are softened but not browned, approximately 10 minutes. Add the tomato paste, stir to coat the other ingredients with the paste, and continue to cook until the paste turns deep red, approximately 5 minutes.

Add the cream, milk, and bouquet garni. Continue cooking until the liquid is reduced by half, 20 to 25 minutes. Add the rice and parsley and continue cooking for 10 minutes. Remove the bouquet garni.

Use tongs or a slotted spoon to remove the lobster claws and shells. Puree the soup in batches in a food processor fitted with the steel blade. Strain and season with 1 teaspoon salt and ½ teaspoon pepper. Finish by stirring in the sherry vinegar and lemon zest. Taste and add more vinegar and/or zest, if necessary.

BREAK POINT
The bisque can be cooled, covered, and refrigerated for up to 24 hours. Refrigerate the lobster meat in a separate container. Reheat the soup gently before proceeding.

To serve, divide the lobster meat among 6 soup bowls. Pour the hot bisque over the lobster and serve.

SEAFOOD SOUP
WITH **SCALLOPS, SQUID,** AND **LOBSTER**

SERVES 6 TO 8 AS A FIRST COURSE OR 4 TO 6 AS A MAIN COURSE

This is my version of the San Francisco–style seafood stew called cioppino. It's very spicy and brawny, a big, satisfying meal in a bowl that matches shellfish with intense spices like coriander and cumin. The two-step process—you make a broth, then add vegetables and shellfish to it—offers an obvious and convenient break point that you should take advantage of.

4 BAY LEAVES

I LEMON, THINLY SLICED

I TABLESPOON BLACK PEPPERCORNS

¼ CUP WHITE WINE VINEGAR

I LOBSTER, I¼ POUNDS

¼ CUP PLUS 2 TABLESPOONS CORN OIL OR OTHER NEUTRAL OIL SUCH AS GRAPESEED OR CANOLA

I MEDIUM ONION, HALF ROUGHLY CHOPPED, HALF FINELY DICED

¾ CUP PEELED, ROUGHLY CHOPPED IDAHO OR RUSSET POTATO PLUS I CUP FINELY DICED POTATO (FROM ABOUT 2 MEDIUM POTATOES)

I CELERY STALK, HALF ROUGHLY CHOPPED, HALF FINELY DICED

2 TABLESPOONS SMASHED GARLIC CLOVES (FROM ABOUT 4 CLOVES)

I TABLESPOON GROUND CORIANDER

I TABLESPOON GROUND FENNEL SEEDS

I TABLESPOON SWEET SPANISH PAPRIKA

I TEASPOON GROUND CUMIN

I TEASPOON DRIED OREGANO

I TEASPOON DRY MUSTARD

¼ CUP PERNOD

¼ CUP DRY WHITE WINE

PEEL OF ½ ORANGE

2 PLUM TOMATOES, ROUGHLY CHOPPED

KOSHER SALT

Pour 10 cups water into a large, heavy-bottomed pot. Add the bay leaves, lemon slices, peppercorns, and vinegar and bring to a boil over high heat. As the water is coming to a boil, fill a large bowl halfway with ice water. Add the lobster (see page 71) to the boiling liquid and cook for 8 minutes. Use tongs to transfer the lobster to the ice water to stop the cooking.

Once cooled, separate the lobster tail and claws from the body. Use a mallet or the back of a heavy kitchen knife to crack the claws and "knuckles" of the lobster and remove the meat. Lay the tail on a flat surface and cut it open lengthwise. Catch all the juices, the tomalley, and the meat in a small bowl. Remove and discard the intestinal tract and stomach (the sac located behind the eyes). Dice the meat into ½-inch chunks and set aside. Gather all the shell and shell fragments and cut them into pieces about 1 inch square with a large, heavy knife.

Heat 3 tablespoons of the corn oil in a heavy-bottomed soup pot set over medium-high heat. Add the roughly chopped onion, roughly chopped potato, roughly chopped celery, and the garlic and cook until softened but not browned, 5 to 6 minutes. Add the lobster shell pieces and cook until bright red and fragrant, 6 to 7 minutes, stirring with a wooden spoon and using it to press on the shells to extract their flavor.

(CONTINUED)

I CUP FINELY DICED FENNEL

I CUP FINELY DICED CARROTS

8 OUNCES BAY SCALLOPS (ABOUT
I CUP)

6 OUNCES CLEANED BABY SQUID FROM
ABOUT IO OUNCES UNCLEANED, CUT
INTO THIN RINGS

PREMIUM EXTRA VIRGIN OLIVE OIL

TO DRINK
OAKY/FULL-BODIED WHITE
LIGHT-BODIED BEER

Add the coriander, ground fennel, paprika, cumin, oregano, and mustard. Stir and cook until the spices are lightly toasted and fragrant, 2 to 3 minutes. Add the Pernod, wine, orange peel, tomatoes, and 2 tablespoons salt and cook, stirring, for 3 minutes.

Pour in 10 cups water, bring to a boil over high heat, then lower the heat and simmer, stirring occasionally, for 1¼ hours.

Remove the pot from the heat and strain the liquid through a fine-mesh strainer set over a bowl, pressing down to extract as much flavorful liquid as possible. Discard the solids. You should have about 7 cups of broth.

BREAK POINT
The broth can be cooled, covered, and refrigerated for up to 24 hours. Refrigerate the cooked, cooled lobster meat separately, wrapping it snugly in plastic wrap.

Heat the remaining 3 tablespoons corn oil in a heavy-bottomed soup pot set over medium-high heat. Add the finely diced celery, finely diced onion, finely diced potato, finely diced fennel, and carrots and cook until softened but not browned, stirring constantly, 7 to 8 minutes.

Add the broth, bring to a boil over high heat, then lower the heat and simmer for 1 hour. Add the scallops, squid, and lobster meat and poach in the soup for 1 to 2 minutes.

To serve, ladle the soup into individual bowls and drizzle each serving with extra virgin olive oil.

MAIN COURSES

(CONTINUED)

STEAKS

IN THE KITCHEN

Okay, we've had our cocktails, our cocktail food, our salad and soup. Everyone's on their second or third glass of wine or bottle of beer, and the get-together is in full swing. It's showtime, which means it's time to fire up the grill.

Of all the cooking techniques, grilling is far and away the one most closely associated with steakhouses, because the high heat of a grill is the most reliable way of producing the elusive char that we all crave. But New American steakhouse cooking is about more than just beef. Think about it: There's no beef in the appetizers at a traditional steakhouse, which tend toward shellfish and salads. And all steakhouses offer something for the non-beef-eater—fish, poultry, and other types of meat—presented in steakhouse fashion with attention-grabbing, Fred Flintstone–size cuts and big, un-shy flavors.

This chapter is about more than just beef as well. Grilling is truly a one-of-a-kind way to bring complex flavor to anything from fruits and vegetables to fish and, of course, types of meat other than beef. When grilled over charcoal, the fats and juices of foods drip down to the coals below, and their essence is returned to them in the smoke that rises from those coals and helps form the char.

Before we get into the individual recipes, allow me to share what I know about grilling.

ON THE GRILL

Let's start with the obvious: if you want to grill great food, you've got to have a great grill, which doesn't necessarily mean an expensive one. In fact, I don't believe in spending an exorbitant amount of money on a grill. This is a machine that will be kept outdoors for at least half the year, if not year-round, which means it's subject to the elements. So spend accordingly.

I don't recommend any particular size or shape, though I do believe in obtaining the largest grill that will fit your space and budget. The more generous the surface area, the more room you have to move cooking (or cooked) foods around, keeping some over the hot spot, some over indirect heat, and holding finished foods off to the side, where they're kept warm by the ambient heat. For charcoal grills, one of the most advantageous features is an adjustable coal bed that allows you to modulate the proximity of the food to the heat source. If you have a big enough grill, that adjustable coal bed almost becomes obsolete because you can move food from side to side rather than moving the coal bed up and down.

CARING FOR YOUR GRILL

One of the most important responsibilities of any grill owner is keeping the grill scrupulously clean. This is true of both charcoal and gas grills, both of which have vents that allow all-important oxygen to flow freely through the fire pit. Depending on how often you use your grill, you should take it apart and clean all the parts and surfaces with soapy water once or twice per season. And you should use a brush to scrub the grates clean after every use. Ditto the burners on a gas grill, which need to be kept free of any excess grease or buildup so the fire can burn as hot as possible.

SET FOR SUCCESS

Just as having all of your ingredients and cooking vessels lined up and ready to go is the key to success in the kitchen, having all of your equipment at the ready is crucial to grilling. At a minimum, have the following equipment, much of which you can read about on pages 18–20, within arm's reach: a grill brush; long, stainless-steel tongs (not a meat fork, which doesn't offer enough control); a rag or kitchen towel to be used to "season" the grill with oil before placing the meat on the grill; an instant-read thermometer, unless you have an innate sense of doneness; and a clean tray to which you can remove the steaks from the grill when they're done. Play around with the best place to keep these items.

CHARCOAL OR GAS?

Purists will tell you that charcoal grills are the only way to go, but there are a lot of factors that make gas grills desirable as well. First, there's no skill required to light a gas grill; you just turn the knob and start cooking. Second, you can regulate the temperature with remarkable ease. Truth be told, I actually prefer a gas grill at home; there's no denying that you sacrifice some flavor, but their user-friendliness is very appealing.

Whatever grill you purchase, there's no better lesson than actually cooking on it. Grills are like any other piece of cooking equipment; each brand and model varies, and each cook will respond to it differently. So you need to spend time getting to know yours and how it works to develop a feel for it. In other words, get out there and start grilling.

CHARCOAL GRILLS. Most people feel that using hardwood charcoal is the only way to go. The choice of which type of wood is a personal one and is completely subjective. The three most popular options are hickory, cherry, and apple.

There are a number of ways to build a fire in a charcoal grill. By far, the easiest is using a chimney starter, a metal cylinder that's open on both ends and has a heat-resistant wood or rubberized handle on its side. To use a chimney starter, fill the canister with charcoal and stuff newspaper into the cavity on the underside of the chimney. Light the newspaper and rest the chimney on the grill grate for 5 to 10 minutes. As the paper burns, the coals will begin to turn a bright red-orange color. At that point, you carefully dump them into the grill's kettle and add more charcoal as necessary.

If you prefer not to use a charcoal starter, there are other ways to go. One is to squirt some lighter fluid on the coals and then carefully light them. Despite its reputation for being a way to "cheat" and an element that will adversely flavor food, lighter fluid is actually rather benign; it always works, and the unsavory flavor cooks out. Just be sure never to use it on already burning coals. Another option is an electric starter, a device that you set in the coal pit with the coals that emits enough heat to set them aflame. As with a lot of grilling decisions, the way you choose to light your fire is a matter of personal preference. There's no right or wrong method; if the food tastes good when you're done cooking, then you made a fine choice.

Although we all picture flames shooting up out of a grill, most of the time that's not the best way to cook. In reality, we usually want to grill over a flameless fire. To achieve this, start by using your tongs to pile up the hot coals. When they're about half white, after 15 to 20 minutes, use the tongs to spread them out to one side of the kettle, leaving the other side cool. Cover the grill with the vent open and let the coals burn for 3 to 5 minutes to build up the intense heat that will cause foods to sear. Let the coals burn down until they're covered with a layer of white ash, which generally takes 30 to 45 minutes.

A common and effective way to determine when the grill is ready is to hold your hand about 6 inches over the grate. If you can keep it there for more than 5 seconds, the grill isn't hot enough and you probably need to add more coals. If you cannot keep it there for 5 seconds, then it's still too hot. When you can keep it there for just about 5 seconds exactly, get grilling.

GAS GRILLS. I don't have a lot to say about gas grills, which actually says about all you need to know. They're not much more complicated than an outdoor stove would be. A gas grill saves you the time and effort of building a fire, and ensures the same, controllable flame every single time. The trade-off is that you don't get the depth of flavor produced by the interaction of fire, fat, charcoal, and food.

A few pieces of gas-grill advice: if you opt for a gas grill, select one with sealed, stainless-steel burners; they generate the most heat and are more durable than others. (Often they come with diffusers that keep food and grease from coating the grill jets, also a good thing.) Another desirable feature is a burner on the side, which allows you to warm sauces and reheat dishes to be served alongside the grilled food. It's also a good idea to keep a spare propane tank on hand so you're always good to go. As with a charcoal grill, leave the lid closed for some time before placing food on the grate, to build the inside temperature and let the grates get very hot.

COOKING ON THE GRILL

One of the most important considerations in grilling takes place before you get to the grill: meats and fish need to come to room temperature; otherwise, they will remain cold at the center, even if the outside is fully cooked. Take them out of the refrigerator, cover loosely with plastic wrap, and let stand at room temperature for 30 to 40 minutes.

Whether using a gas or charcoal grill, it must be seasoned after being turned on (gas grill) or after the coals have been knocked down (charcoal grill): Fold or bunch up your rag or kitchen towel, pick it up with long tongs, dip it in oil, lean away, and use it to season the grill with a swipe of cooking oil. Work quickly to avoid flare-ups and/or igniting the rag.

If using a gas grill, wave your hand over the grill to find the "hot spot" of the grill; that's where you put the food you're going to grill.

If a flare-up should occur while grilling, don't drag food across the grate; you'll only continue to feed and spread the fire as fat continues to drip from the food. Instead, use tongs to lift and move the food to another spot in one deft movement.

I hope you'll use the sauces and sides in this book to accompany grilled foods, but even if you're serving them on their own, keep in mind that there are a number of ways to finish them between the grill and the table. My two favorites are brushing on some Clarified Butter (page 16) or sprinkling a little sea salt over them just before serving to really draw out their flavor.

THE CAST-IRON ALTERNATIVE

At home, it's difficult to use a broiler in place of a grill; because of the relatively low BTUs of a residential stove, the broiler doesn't get very hot. It browns the top but it just doesn't put out enough heat to adequately sear a piece of meat before it starts to overcook the inside.

Using a cast-iron skillet, however, produces results that are surprisingly close to grilling outdoors. Cast iron is really the only way to get this close to a grilling result indoors. Here's why: with a cast-iron skillet, you do not put cooking fat into the pan. (When you cook with a sauté pan, you usually put the cooking oil in the pan and get both very hot before you cook. You cannot get the sauté pan and oil hot enough to properly cook a thick steak before the pan begins to smoke and the oil ignites.)

With cast iron, you oil what you are going to cook, so you can put a well-seasoned cast-iron pan on the stove burner and allow it to become very hot with no fear of a flame-up. And cast iron's temperature doesn't drop when you add food to it the way a steel pan's does, unless you overcrowd it. A good rule of thumb is that the area of a cast-iron pan should be twice that of what's being cooked.

There are a few pitfalls to cooking with cast iron: One is that whatever you cook doesn't take on the same complex flavor you get in the char of a grill because those fats and juices don't make the trip down to the coals and back. A second drawback is that meats cooked at high heat throw as much smoke indoors as they do outdoors; it can be tough to manage. The solution is ventilation, ventilation, ventilation. A properly ventilated stove, or proximity to an open window (preferably with a fan blowing the smoke in its direction) is crucial. You might even want to turn off your smoke detector when you start. Just be sure to turn it back on as soon as you're done.

Finally, cast iron can be a pain to clean because using water can cause a hot pan to crack and the pan should be cleaned when still hot. My preferred method of cleaning cast iron is to use a combination of coarse salt and shortening, such as Crisco. When you're done cooking and all of the food is out of the pan, cover the surface of the hot pan with salt. Let the salt cool in there, then turn it out into a sink, using a kitchen towel to wipe it out, treating the salt like a scouring/cleaning agent. Add a few tablespoons of shortening to the pan and wipe it down, working out any cooked-on food with additional salt. This will leave you with a clean, well-seasoned pan.

As for cooking times, a good rule of thumb is to add about 10 percent to the recipe's time if moving from an outdoor grill to a cast-iron pan.

To cook in a cast-iron pan, preheat it over medium-high heat for at least 15 minutes. Oil the meat, not the skillet, so you can get it very hot without danger of a flare-up. Once the pan is hot, add the meat and let it sear, turning it only after the first side is nicely charred.

When cooking meat, cast iron offers you a break point: you can sear the meat in the pan, remove it, let it cool slightly, and refrigerate it for up to 2 hours, then reheat and finish it on a baking sheet in an oven preheated to 400°F. (Reheating times will vary based on the size and thickness of the cut and on desired doneness; for best results, use an instant-read thermometer and refer to the temperatures on page 122.)

GRILLED MAINE LOBSTER
WITH **ORANGE-TARRAGON BUTTER**

SERVES 2

One of my favorite ways to cook lobster is on the grill, melting an herb butter into the meat. The butter gets trapped by the shell, causing the flavors to really integrate. Here, the butter features tarragon, a real go-to herb for lobster, and orange, which highlights the sweetness of the flesh. The lobster is also delicious paired with New York Strip Steak (page 124), a modern surf and turf.

This recipe asks you to kill the lobster before cooking it. It might sound unkind, but it's actually the most humane option because it kills the lobster instantly.

8 TABLESPOONS (I STICK) UNSALTED BUTTER, SOFTENED AT ROOM TEMPERATURE

2 TEASPOONS CHOPPED FRESH TARRAGON LEAVES

I TEASPOON CHOPPED FRESH CHIVES

2 TEASPOONS PERNOD OR GRAND MARNIER

2 TEASPOONS FINELY GRATED ORANGE ZEST

I TEASPOON PULVERIZED GARLIC (SEE PAGE 2I)

KOSHER SALT

FRESHLY GROUND BLACK PEPPER

2 MAINE LOBSTERS, I½ POUNDS EACH

2 TABLESPOONS CORN OIL OR OTHER NEUTRAL OIL SUCH AS GRAPESEED OR CANOLA

TO DRINK
CRISP/FRESH WHITE
LIGHT/FLORAL WHITE

Put the softened butter in a small bowl and add the tarragon, chives, Pernod, orange zest, garlic, ½ teaspoon salt, and ¼ teaspoon pepper. Stir with a rubber spatula until well integrated. Refrigerate for up to 2 days or freeze for up to 2 months. Let thaw, soften, and melt slightly before using.

Prepare your grill for grilling (see pages 96–100).

Plunge a large kitchen knife into each lobster's head right behind the eyes and pull it down like a lever to quickly kill it.

Remove the claws from the lobster and crack the claws and knuckles with the back of a heavy kitchen knife. Split the lobsters in half lengthwise. Remove the small sac in the front of the head and discard it, leaving the tomalley and any roe intact. Lightly coat the cut side of the lobster halves and cracked claws with the oil.

Put the lobster halves on the grill, cut side up, and grill until the shells turn slightly red, approximately 3 minutes. Move the lobster halves over indirect heat, leaving the cracked claws over the hot spot. Generously brush the cut sides of the lobster halves and claws with the orange-herb butter.

Close the grill lid and cook for another 3 minutes. Use tongs to remove the lobsters from the grill. Put the cracked claws in a bowl and toss to generously coat with half of the remaining orange butter. Brush the lobster tails with the other half.

To serve, arrange the lobster pieces on a platter or divide them among individual plates.

SEAWEED-STEAMED MAINE LOBSTER
AND **GRILLED CORN ON THE COB**

SERVES 2

This is my preferred method of preparing the classic, all-American lobster cookout with grilled corn, drawn butter, and lemon wedges. By wrapping the lobster in wet seaweed, you steam it as it grills, resulting in a fresh, clean, slightly oceanic flavor. As with the previous lobster recipe, this can become half of a surf-and-turf meal paired with grilled New York Strip Steak (page 124).

3 POUNDS SEAWEED (AVAILABLE FROM SEAFOOD STORES; CALL FIRST, THEY MIGHT NEED TO SPECIAL-ORDER IT) OR HUSKS FROM 6 EARS CORN

2 MAINE LOBSTERS, 1½ POUNDS EACH

½ CUP CLARIFIED BUTTER (PAGE 16)

GRILL-ROASTED SWEET CORN ON THE COB WITH SUN-DRIED TOMATO BUTTER (PAGE 149)

LEMON WEDGES, FOR SERVING

TO DRINK
OAKY/FULL-BODIED WHITE
BLOND BEER

Cover the seaweed with cold water in a large bowl and let soak for 2 hours. (If using corn husks, soak for just 1 hour.)

Prepare your grill for grilling (see pages 96–100).

Plunge a large kitchen knife into each lobster's head right behind the eyes and pull it down like a lever to quickly kill it. Crack the claws and knuckles with the back of a heavy kitchen knife and leave the claws attached.

Lay half of the seaweed on a flat surface. Set 1 lobster on the seaweed and roll it snugly in the seaweed. Repeat with the second lobster and the remaining seaweed. (If using corn husks, see below.)

Set the seaweed-wrapped lobsters over medium, indirect heat, cover the grill, and cook until the shells are bright red, 8 to 10 minutes. Remove the lobsters from the seaweed and set them aside.

(If using corn husks, remove them from the water and squeeze them by hand to extract as much water as possible; you don't want them to dampen the charcoal or flame when set on the grill. Arrange a thick layer of about half the husks on the grill directly over the hot spot. Set the lobsters on top and cover with the remaining husks. Cover the grill and cook until the shells are bright red and the lobster claws no longer flop limply when the lobster is lifted, approximately 15 minutes.)

To serve, split the lobster tails with a kitchen knife, arrange on a platter, and serve with the butter, corn, and lemon wedges passed on the side.

TUNA LOIN
with JALAPEÑO-CORN CUSTARDS and MARINATED SCALLIONS

SERVES 4

This main course takes tuna in a southwestern direction, coating it with a cumin-coriander dry rub and pairing it with a corn custard and grilled, marinated scallions. Make the custards first, or bake them as you're grilling the scallions and tuna so that everything is ready at the same time.

4 SCALLIONS, WHITE PART ONLY

3 TABLESPOONS CORN OIL OR OTHER NEUTRAL OIL SUCH AS GRAPESEED OR CANOLA

KOSHER SALT

FRESHLY GROUND BLACK PEPPER

2 TEASPOONS GROUND CORIANDER

2 TEASPOONS GROUND CUMIN

$1^{3}/_{4}$ POUNDS YELLOWFIN TUNA LOIN, CUT INTO 2 BY 2 BY 5-INCH PIECES (BUY FOUR 7-OUNCE PORTIONS OR I LOIN THAT CAN BE SLICED ACCORDINGLY)

I TEASPOON YUZU JUICE, OR $1/_2$ TEASPOONS FRESHLY SQUEEZED LEMON JUICE PLUS $1/_2$ TEASPOONS GRAPEFRUIT JUICE

2 TABLESPOONS EXTRA VIRGIN OLIVE OIL

I TABLESPOON SOY SAUCE

JALAPEÑO CORN CUSTARDS (RECIPE FOLLOWS)

TO DRINK
OAKY/FULL-BODIED WHITE

Prepare your grill for grilling (see pages 96–100).

Brush the scallions lightly with 1 tablespoon of the corn oil and season to taste with salt and pepper. Grill them until lightly charred, approximately 4 minutes, turning them as they cook. Remove from the grill and set aside to cool.

Make a dry rub by stirring together the coriander, cumin, 2 teaspoons black pepper, and 2 teaspoons salt in a small bowl. Spread the mixture out on a plate. Pour the remaining 2 tablespoons corn oil out on another plate. One by one, dredge the tuna pieces in the oil, then roll them in the dry rub, pressing down to make sure the spices adhere to the fish.

Put the tuna on the grill and grill until the spices are nicely toasted and the tuna is warmed through, approximately 3 minutes per side.

Slice the scallions crosswise into thin slices and put them in a bowl. Add the yuzu juice, extra virgin olive oil, and soy sauce, and toss.

To serve, slice the tuna into ¼-inch slices and divide among 4 dinner plates. Put a custard and some scallion salad alongside the tuna on each plate. Drizzle any vinaigrette remaining in the scallion's bowl around the plate.

JALAPEÑO-CORN CUSTARDS

2 TABLESPOONS CORN OIL OR OTHER
NEUTRAL OIL SUCH AS GRAPESEED
OR CANOLA

$\frac{1}{4}$ MEDIUM ONION, DICED

I CUP SWEET CORN KERNELS, FRESH
OR FROZEN

KOSHER SALT

I CUP HEAVY CREAM

4 LARGE EGG YOLKS

I JALAPEÑO, SEEDED AND FINELY DICED

I LARGE GARLIC CLOVE, PULVERIZED
(SEE PAGE 21)

$\frac{1}{8}$ TEASPOON GROUND CORIANDER

$\frac{1}{8}$ TEASPOON GROUND CUMIN

FRESHLY GROUND BLACK PEPPER

UNSALTED BUTTER FOR GREASING
THE RAMEKINS

Heat the oil in a sauté pan set over medium-high heat. Add the onion and sauté until softened but not browned, approximately 4 minutes. Remove from the heat and set aside to cool.

Put the corn in a large pot, add enough water to cover (about $\frac{1}{2}$ cup), and season with 1 tablespoon salt. Set the pot over high heat and bring the water to a boil. Boil until the kernels are tender, 3 to 5 minutes, then transfer the corn to a blender and pulse to a coarse, thickened mixture.

Preheat the oven to 350°F.

Stir together the cream, yolks, jalapeño, onion, garlic, coriander, cumin, $\frac{1}{4}$ teaspoon pepper, and corn puree in a bowl. Butter four 6-ounce ramekins, arrange them on a rimmed baking sheet without crowding, and divide the custard among the ramekins.

Bake the custards for 20 minutes. Check them throughout the cooking process to ensure that the timing is right. (The height and diameter of the ramekins can affect the cooking time of the custards.) They are done when a toothpick inserted in the center of a custard comes out clean and the custard feels firm to the touch. Run a sharp, thin-bladed knife around the perimeter of the ramekins, invert each of them on a dinner plate, and unmold.

GRILLED SALMON
WITH **BUTTERED LEEKS** AND **SHIITAKE MUSHROOMS**

SERVES 4

In this dish, rich, fatty salmon is matched by luxurious glazed leeks and earthy mushrooms, all of it offset with a lemon and herb salad. It's a surprisingly easy dish to cook, with a broad range of well-balanced flavors.

Serve this with Vegetable-Stuffed Red Ripe Tomatoes (page 152).

2 TABLESPOONS UNSALTED BUTTER

2 LEEKS, WHITE PART ONLY, HALVED LENGTHWISE AND CUT INTO SEMICIRCULAR RINGS ABOUT $\frac{1}{4}$ INCH WIDE, WELL WASHED UNDER COLD WATER TO REMOVE ANY DIRT OR SAND

KOSHER SALT

FRESHLY GROUND BLACK PEPPER

$\frac{1}{4}$ CUP CORN OIL OR OTHER NEUTRAL OIL SUCH AS GRAPESEED OR CANOLA

2 TABLESPOONS MINCED SHALLOTS

2 CUPS JULIENNED SHIITAKE MUSHROOM CAPS (FROM ABOUT 15 SHIITAKES)

2 TABLESPOONS CHOPPED FRESH FLAT-LEAF PARSLEY LEAVES PLUS $\frac{1}{4}$ CUP WHOLE LEAVES

$\frac{1}{4}$ CUP FRESH BASIL LEAVES, EACH TORN INTO 2 OR 3 PIECES

$\frac{1}{4}$ CUP FRESH CHIVES CUT INTO $1\frac{1}{4}$-INCH PEGS (SEE PAGE 21)

$\frac{1}{4}$ CUP CHOPPED FRESH DILL FRONDS

2 TABLESPOONS EXTRA VIRGIN OLIVE OIL

2 TEASPOONS FRESHLY SQUEEZED LEMON JUICE

4 BONELESS SALMON STEAKS, ABOUT 7 OUNCES EACH

TO DRINK
CRISP/FRESH WHITE
SMOOTH/MEDIUM-BODIED RED

Melt the butter in a heavy-bottomed saucepan set over medium heat. Add the leeks and 1 cup water, season to taste with salt and pepper, and cook, stirring frequently, until the leeks are softened and coated with a buttery glaze. Set aside.

Heat 2 tablespoons of the corn oil in a large, heavy-bottomed sauté pan set over medium-high heat. Add the shallots and sauté for 20 seconds, then add the mushrooms and cook until tender, 4 to 5 minutes. Add the chopped parsley and toss to incorporate with the mushrooms, then add the mushroom mixture to the buttered leeks. Taste and adjust the seasoning with salt and pepper if necessary. Cover and keep warm.

Prepare your grill for grilling (see pages 96–100) or use a cast-iron pan.

About 10 minutes before cooking the salmon, put the parsley leaves, basil, chives, and dill in a small bowl with the olive oil, lemon juice, ¼ teaspoon salt, and ⅛ teaspoon pepper. Gently toss.

Rub the salmon steaks with the remaining 2 tablespoons corn oil and season to taste on both sides with salt and pepper.

Grill the salmon over the hot spot until nice grill marks form and the steaks are warmed through but still rare in the center, approximately 3 minutes per side. Use tongs to remove the salmon from the grill. Set the sauté pan with the leeks and mushrooms over medium heat, either indoors or on the grill, for a minute or so to re-warm them.

To serve, put a portion of the leeks and mushrooms on individual plates, or a long platter, cover with the salmon, and top with a portion of the herb salad.

MARINATED SWORDFISH

WITH **FRESH HERB BUTTER**

SERVES 4

There's a universal lesson in this dish: use a compound butter to add quick, potent flavor to fish or meat after it's been cooked. A compound butter is a butter that's enriched with herbs and lemon juice and/or wine, then firmed up in the refrigerator or freezer before being cut into pieces and set atop cooked food. As the heat of the food melts the butter, the flavors are unleashed. Here, a compound butter is set atop grilled swordfish. The cooked-in flavor of the fish and fresh, butter-based accents come together beautifully.

Serve this with Stewed Tomatoes (page 153) and/or Lobster Mashed Potatoes (page 162).

½ CUP EXTRA VIRGIN OLIVE OIL

ZEST AND JUICE OF 1 LEMON

4 SWORDFISH STEAKS, 8 OUNCES EACH, CENTER CUT, 1 INCH THICK

KOSHER SALT

FRESHLY GROUND BLACK PEPPER

FRESH HERB BUTTER (RECIPE FOLLOWS)

TO DRINK
SMOOTH/MEDIUM-BODIED RED
AMBER BEER

Prepare your grill for grilling (see pages 96–100) or preheat a cast-iron pan.

Stir together the oil and lemon zest and juice in a small bowl. Pour out onto a plate and turn the steaks in the mixture. Season on both sides with 1 tablespoon salt and 2 teaspoons pepper.

Grill the swordfish over the hot spot until nice grill marks form and the fish is warmed through and medium at the center, approximately 3 minutes per side. Use tongs to transfer 1 steak to each of 4 dinner plates. As soon as the swordfish comes off the grill, place 1 tablespoon of the butter on top of each portion. Allow the butter to melt slightly before serving.

FRESH HERB BUTTER

MAKES ABOUT ⅓ CUP

4 TABLESPOONS (½ STICK) UNSALTED BUTTER, SOFTENED AT ROOM TEMPERATURE

I TEASPOON PULVERIZED GARLIC (SEE PAGE 21)

I TEASPOON MINCED SHALLOTS

I TEASPOON MINCED FRESH FLAT-LEAF PARSLEY LEAVES

I TEASPOON MINCED FRESH THYME LEAVES

I TEASPOON MINCED FRESH OREGANO LEAVES

I TEASPOON MINCED FRESH CHIVES

I TEASPOON FRESHLY SQUEEZED LEMON JUICE

½ TEASPOON KOSHER SALT

¼ TEASPOON FRESHLY GROUND BLACK PEPPER

Combine the butter with all of the other ingredients in a bowl and stir well with a rubber spatula to evenly incorporate them. Put the butter in a small dish or ramekin, cover with plastic wrap, and refrigerate until firm, approximately 1 hour.

The butter can be refrigerated for up to 3 days, or rolled into a log, wrapped in plastic wrap, and frozen for up to 2 months.

LEMON-PEPPER
MARINATED CHICKEN
with GRILLED ASPARAGUS

SERVES 4

Sometimes the most basic dishes can be the most satisfying, like this lemon-pepper chicken with asparagus. The ingredients and result are very familiar, and that's exactly why I love them. I think of this as comfort food from the grill.

Serve this with Tabbouleh Salad with Lemon and Cucumber (page 147).

2 TABLESPOONS FINELY GRATED LEMON ZEST PLUS JUICE OF 1 LEMON

2 TABLESPOONS CHOPPED FRESH THYME LEAVES PLUS 4 THYME SPRIGS

2 TABLESPOONS COARSELY CRACKED BLACK PEPPER

1 TABLESPOON PULVERIZED GARLIC (SEE PAGE 21)

1/2 CUP PLUS 2 TABLESPOONS EXTRA VIRGIN OLIVE OIL

KOSHER SALT

2 WHOLE CHICKENS, 3 POUNDS EACH, QUARTERED, BACKBONE REMOVED

1 LEMON, THINLY SLICED

1/2 CUP DRY WHITE WINE

1 POUND JUMBO ASPARAGUS

FRESHLY GROUND BLACK PEPPER

TO DRINK
OAKY/FULL-BODIED WHITE
SPICY RED
BLOND BEER

In a bowl, stir together the lemon zest and juice, chopped thyme, coarsely cracked pepper, garlic, 2 tablespoons extra virgin olive oil, and 1 teaspoon salt.

Put the chicken on a flat surface, skin side up. Gently lift the skin away from the meat on each piece, using your fingers to create a pocket at the breast and another at the thigh. Spoon about 1 tablespoon of the mixture under the skin near the breast and about 2 teaspoons at the thigh. Put the chicken in a shallow roasting pan, skin side up.

Squeeze the lemon slices over the chicken and place them and the thyme sprigs on top.

In a small bowl, mix 1/4 cup of the extra virgin olive oil with the wine and drizzle the mixture over the chicken in the roasting pan. Cover with plastic wrap and refrigerate for 2 to 3 hours.

BREAK POINT
The chicken can marinate overnight.

When ready to cook, prepare your grill for grilling (see pages 96–100).

Using a vegetable peeler, lightly peel away the outer skin from the asparagus from about 1 inch below the tips toward the stem ends.

Lay the asparagus on a cutting board and line up the tips evenly. Cut about 1 1/2 inches away from the stem ends and discard the trimmings. Put the trimmed asparagus in a bowl and dress with the remaining ¼ cup olive oil, 2 teaspoons salt, and 1 teaspoon black pepper. Bring the asparagus and chickens to the grill.

Remove the chicken from the marinade and season with a total of 1 tablespoon salt and 2 teaspoons black pepper. Put the chicken skin side down on a medium-high spot on the grill. Grill until the skin is golden brown, 6 to 8 minutes. If the grill flares up, move the chicken to a cooler spot on the grill until the flare-up subsides.

Turn the chicken over and move them off the direct heat to a cooler spot. Close the lid and grill for an additional 20 minutes over low-medium heat. Check the chicken by inserting a small knife into the thighs. The juices should run clear. (You can also check by ensuring that the temperature at the thickest part of the chicken reads 160°F on an instant-read thermometer.) When the pieces are done, transfer the chicken to a serving platter and let rest.

While the chicken is resting, grill the seasoned asparagus on the low-medium spot on the grill for 5 to 6 minutes, turning the pieces to char and brown all over.

Put the grilled asparagus on a serving tray and serve alongside the chicken.

GRILLED HALF CHICKEN
WITH **AROMATIC VEGETABLES**

SERVES 4

This dish is all about the marinade, a blend of garlic, fennel, wine, lemons, and herbs in which the chicken is marinated overnight, then grilled. The aromatic vegetables are stewed with butter and water to create a mix of glazed vegetables in one fell swoop; given how big the flavors are, you'll be amazed at how easy it was to create them. Keep this side dish in mind as an accompaniment to other poultry dishes.

Serve this with Black Truffle Creamed Spinach (page 154) or Gruyère Potato Gratin (page 166).

³/₄ CUP EXTRA VIRGIN OLIVE OIL

2 HEADS GARLIC, HALVED HORIZONTALLY

¹/₂ MEDIUM WHITE ONION, ROUGHLY CHOPPED

I TABLESPOON FENNEL SEEDS

3 BAY LEAVES

I TEASPOON CRACKED BLACK PEPPER

I¹/₂ CUPS DRY WHITE WINE

2 LEMONS, EACH SLICED INTO 5 OR 6 SLICES

¹/₂ CUP ROUGHLY CHOPPED FRESH FLAT-LEAF PARSLEY LEAVES

6 FRESH THYME SPRIGS

4 FRESH ROSEMARY SPRIGS

KOSHER SALT

2 WHOLE CHICKENS, 3 POUNDS EACH, HALVED, BACKBONE AND BREAST CARTILAGE REMOVED, TRIMMED OF ANY EXCESS FAT AND SKIN AT THE TOP OF THE BREAST

AROMATIC VEGETABLES (RECIPE FOLLOWS)

TO DRINK
OAKY/FULL-BODIED WHITE
BLOND BEER

Heat the oil in a large, heavy-bottomed saucepan over medium-high heat. Add the garlic halves, cut side down, and brown for 2 to 3 minutes. Add the onion and cook until slightly softened, 1 to 2 minutes. Add the fennel seeds, bay leaves, and cracked black pepper and toast for 1 minute. Add the wine, 1¹/₂ cups water, the lemons, parsley, thyme, rosemary, and 1 tablespoon salt. Bring to a boil and let boil for 6 minutes. Remove the pan from the heat and let cool to room temperature.

Cover the pan and refrigerate the mixture until chilled, approximately 1 hour.

Put the chicken halves skin side down in a single layer in a large casserole and pour the marinade over them, making sure they are submerged. Cover and marinate overnight.

BREAK POINT
The chicken can be refrigerated for up to 24 hours.

When ready to proceed, prepare your grill for grilling (see pages 96–100) or use a cast-iron pan.

Grill the chicken skin side down for 4 to 5 minutes to brown, checking frequently to make sure they aren't burning. Turn the chicken over onto the rib-cage side and move to an indirect, medium-high part of the grill. Close the lid and grill for 20 to 25 minutes, periodically lifting the lid to make sure they are not burning. Cook until an instant-read thermometer reads 160°F when inserted in the thickest portion of the thighs.

To serve, put 1 chicken half on each of 4 plates and spoon some vegetables alongside.

AROMATIC VEGETABLES

4 CELERY STALKS, SCRAPED AND CUT CROSSWISE INTO 3-INCH SEGMENTS

2 MEDIUM CARROTS, CUT INTO $\frac{1}{2}$-INCH DISCS

1 MEDIUM WHITE ONION, HALVED LENGTHWISE

2 LEEKS, WHITE PART ONLY, LEFT INTACT AT THE ROOT END AND SPLIT LENGTHWISE, WELL WASHED UNDER COLD WATER TO REMOVE ANY DIRT OR SAND

12 LARGE GARLIC CLOVES, TRIMMED AT THE ROOT END

2 BAY LEAVES

2 TABLESPOONS UNSALTED BUTTER

$1\frac{1}{2}$ TEASPOONS KOSHER SALT

$\frac{1}{2}$ TEASPOON FRESHLY GROUND BLACK PEPPER

Heat all the ingredients with 1 cup water in a large, covered, heavy-bottomed pot over medium heat. Cook until all the vegetables are soft and most of the water has evaporated, approximately 8 minutes. The liquid and butter will create a glaze to coat the vegetables.

The vegetables can be cooled, covered, and refrigerated for up to 24 hours. Reheat by putting the uncovered pot on the grill for 5 to 10 minutes. (If you close the grill, the vegetables will take on a subtle smoky flavor.)

GRILLED CHICKEN PAILLARD
WITH **SMOKED BACON**
AND **MARINATED PORTOBELLO MUSHROOMS**

SERVES 4

Normally, the char flavor of grilled meats is somewhat balanced by the thickness of the cut. This dish takes the opposite tack: the chicken breasts are pounded down, so you really taste the char. Adding to this symphony of smoke are grilled bacon and earthy portobello mushrooms.

Serve this with Michael's Macaroni and Cheese (page 168).

4 SKINLESS, BONELESS CHICKEN BREASTS, ABOUT 6 OUNCES EACH

3 TABLESPOONS PLAIN YOGURT

I TABLESPOON FINELY MINCED SHALLOTS

2 TABLESPOONS PEELED AND FINELY GRATED CUCUMBER

KOSHER SALT

FRESHLY GROUND BLACK PEPPER

½ TEASPOON SWEET SPANISH PAPRIKA

I TEASPOON PULVERIZED GARLIC (SEE PAGE 21) PLUS I TEASPOON FINELY MINCED GARLIC

I TEASPOON FINELY CHOPPED FRESH THYME LEAVES

¼ CUP EXTRA VIRGIN OLIVE OIL

4 SLICES DOUBLE-SMOKED BACON, ¾ INCH THICK

2 PORTOBELLO MUSHROOMS, HALVED

I TABLESPOON SHERRY VINEGAR

TO DRINK
LIGHT/FLORAL WHITE
LIGHT-BODIED BEER

Lay a sheet of plastic wrap on a cutting board. Put 1 chicken breast on the plastic and cover with another sheet. Use a mallet or meat tenderizer to pound the breast to a ¼-inch thickness. Repeat the process until all of the chicken is pounded out.

Stir together the yogurt, shallots, cucumber, 2 teaspoons salt, 1 teaspoon pepper, paprika, pulverized garlic, thyme, and 1 tablespoon of the olive oil in a bowl. Put the chicken breasts in the marinade, cover, and refrigerate for 15 to 20 minutes.

BREAK POINT
The chicken can marinate for up to 2 hours.

Prepare your grill for grilling (see pages 96–100).

Grill the bacon for about 11 minutes, turning once or twice, until browned and crisp. Transfer to a paper-towel-lined plate to drain.

Remove the breasts from the marinade. Grill over high heat until nicely charred and cooked through, approximately 2 minutes per side. Transfer the chicken to a plate and let rest while you grill the mushrooms.

Rub the portobellos with 1 tablespoon extra virgin olive oil, season to taste with salt and pepper, and grill for 4 to 5 minutes, turning once, until lightly browned and softened. Combine the minced garlic, remaining 2 tablespoons olive oil, and sherry vinegar in a small bowl; season to taste with salt and pepper and place the hot grilled mushrooms in the vinaigrette. Let marinate for a few minutes while you plate the chicken and bacon.

Put 1 chicken breast on each of 4 dinner plates. Put a slice of bacon and a marinated mushroom half on each plate.

SCALLION-SESAME
TURKEY BURGER

SERVES 4

Break with tradition and serve this burger without the bread, pairing it instead with a selection of sauces and sides or a simple mixed green salad. This is what we all wish lower-fat turkey burgers tasted like but they rarely do: moist, flavorful, and highly seasoned, thanks in large part to the inclusion of sesame oil and soy sauce.

Serve this with Garlic-Herb French Fries (page 160) or Curried Peas and Corn (page 148).

1½ POUNDS GROUND TURKEY

3 TABLESPOONS WHITE SESAME SEEDS

2 TABLESPOONS SOY SAUCE

½ CUP MINCED SCALLIONS, WHITE AND GREEN PARTS

2 TABLESPOONS MINCED FRESH CILANTRO LEAVES

2 TEASPOONS PULVERIZED GARLIC (SEE PAGE 21)

2 TABLESPOONS SESAME OIL

KOSHER SALT

1¼ CUPS FRESH BREAD CRUMBS

FRESHLY GROUND BLACK PEPPER

3 TABLESPOONS CORN OIL OR OTHER NEUTRAL OIL SUCH AS GRAPESEED OR CANOLA

TO DRINK
LIGHT/FLORAL WHITE
CRISP/FRESH WHITE

Knead together, gently by hand, the turkey, sesame seeds, soy sauce, scallions, cilantro, garlic, sesame oil, 1 teaspoon salt, and the bread crumbs in a bowl. Form into 4 patties about 1 inch thick and 4 inches in diameter.

BREAK POINT
The patties may be refrigerated for 2 hours before grilling or frozen for up to 3 days; layer sheets of wax paper between them and wrap in plastic wrap.

Prepare your grill for grilling (see pages 96–100) or preheat a cast-iron pan.

Season the burgers to taste with salt and pepper. Pour the corn oil on a plate and coat the exterior of the burgers well by dredging them in the oil.

Grill the burgers on the hot spot of the grill until nicely charred and cooked through, approximately 4 minutes per side. Let rest for 2 to 3 minutes before serving on individual plates.

GRILLED DUCK BREAST
WITH **CHARRED TOMATO–SMOKED CHILE SAUCE** AND **TALEGGIO CHEESE**

SERVES 4

Because it's so deliciously rich, duck can coexist with a great number of ingredients and its flavor will still come through loud and clear. In this dish, grilled duck is paired with a sauce of charred tomatoes and smoky chipotle peppers, then topped with a jalapeño and cheese mixture. Pay close attention when grilling the duck; because of its high fat content, this is one of those times when flare-ups are inevitable. The payoff is that as the fat melts away, the skin becomes irresistibly crispy.

Serve this with Batter-Fried Onions (page 158).

4 OUNCES IMPORTED TALEGGIO CHEESE OR MILD BLUE CHEESE, SOFTENED AT ROOM TEMPERATURE

I JALAPEÑO, ROASTED, PEELED, AND FINELY DICED (SEE PAGE 177)

I TABLESPOON PLUS 2 TEASPOONS FINELY CHOPPED FRESH CILANTRO LEAVES

6 PLUM TOMATOES

I TABLESPOON PLUS 2 TEASPOONS CORN OIL OR OTHER NEUTRAL OIL SUCH AS GRAPESEED OR CANOLA

¼ CUP ROUGHLY CHOPPED WHITE ONION

I TEASPOON CHOPPED GARLIC

I TABLESPOON FINELY CHOPPED CANNED CHIPOTLE IN ADOBO

I½ CUPS VEGETABLE STOCK (PAGE 12) OR LOW-SODIUM, STORE-BOUGHT VEGETABLE BROTH

KOSHER SALT

FRESHLY GROUND BLACK PEPPER

I TABLESPOON VEGETABLE OIL, IF COOKING INDOORS

4 BONELESS DUCK BREASTS, ABOUT 12 OUNCES EACH, SKIN SCORED IN A CROSSHATCH PATTERN

In a small bowl, stir together the Taleggio, jalapeño, and 2 teaspoons cilantro. Cover and refrigerate until ready to use.

Prepare your grill for grilling (see pages 96–100) or preheat the broiler.

To make the sauce, gently toss the tomatoes with the 2 teaspoons corn oil in a bowl to coat the tomatoes with the oil. Grill them over high heat on the grill or under the broiler to char the skin, approximately 5 minutes, rotating the tomatoes during cooking to char all over. Roughly chop the tomatoes and set them aside.

Heat the 1 tablespoon corn oil in a heavy-bottomed sauté pan. Add the onion and garlic and sauté until lightly browned, 3 to 4 minutes. Immediately add the tomatoes, chipotle, 1 tablespoon cilantro, stock, 1¼ teaspoons salt, and ¼ teaspoon pepper and cook, stirring, over medium-high heat for 4 to 5 minutes. Transfer the mixture to a blender and puree until smooth.

If cooking indoors put the vegetable oil in a heavy-bottomed sauté pan and preheat over medium heat.

Season the duck breasts with 2 tablespoons salt and 1 tablespoon pepper. If grilling, grill over indirect, medium-high heat, skin side down, for 10 minutes, moving the breasts often to keep them from blackening over the flare-ups. Turn over the duck breasts and grill for an additional 10 minutes over low heat. If cooking indoors, cook the duck breasts in the preheated sauté pan for approximately 10 minutes per side, periodically draining off any fat that accumulates in the pan. When ready, remove from the heat and let rest for 3 to 4 minutes before slicing.

To serve, slice the duck breasts into $\frac{1}{4}$-inch-thick slices. Spoon about one-quarter of the sauce in the center of each of 4 dinner plates and top with slices of duck breast. Crumble the cheese mixture over the duck and serve.

SMOKED CHILE BURGER

SERVES 4

Over the years I've cooked in a number of restaurants that specialized in southwestern food and these burgers call on that experience. If you've ever made beef tacos or enchiladas at home, then you know how well powdered chiles take to ground beef. This burger doubles up on the smoke factor: the char of the grill is complemented by chipotle (smoked jalapeño) chile powder in the burger itself.

By the way, one of the key contributors to a great burger has nothing to do with the cooking: be sure to use a nice, durable roll that won't get soggy when it absorbs the juices. My favorite is an unseeded kaiser roll.

Serve this with Garlic-Parmesan Potato Chips (page 159).

I TABLESPOON CORN OIL OR OTHER NEUTRAL OIL SUCH AS GRAPESEED OR CANOLA

¼ CUP FINELY DICED WHITE ONION

I TO 2 TABLESPOONS CHIPOTLE CHILE POWDER (MCCORMICK AND OTHER BRANDS AVAILABLE IN THE JARRED SPICE SECTION OF WELL-STOCKED SUPERMARKETS AND GOURMET SHOPS)

2 POUNDS PRIME GROUND SIRLOIN

3 GARLIC CLOVES, PULVERIZED (ABOUT I TABLESPOON; SEE PAGE 21)

2 TABLESPOONS STORE-BOUGHT BARBECUE SAUCE

I TABLESPOON WORCESTERSHIRE SAUCE

KOSHER SALT

FRESHLY GROUND BLACK PEPPER

TO DRINK
AMBER BEER

If cooking immediately, prepare your grill for grilling (see pages 96–100) or use a cast-iron pan.

Heat the oil in a small sauté pan set over medium-high heat. Add the onion and sauté until softened but not browned, approximately 4 minutes. Remove the pan from the heat.

Stir the chile powder together with 1 tablespoon water in a small bowl to make a paste. Add the onion and stir to coat with the paste and release the flavor of the chile. Let the mixture cool to room temperature. Add the beef, garlic, barbecue sauce, Worcestershire sauce, and 2 tablespoons salt. Work the mixture by hand to evenly incorporate the ingredients. Divide into 4 burgers, about 1¾ inches thick and 4½ inches in diameter. As you form each burger, depress the center by about ¼ inch with your thumb. (When ground beef cooks, it swells in the center; this indentation will help the beef cook and char evenly.) Do not overwork the mixture.

BREAK POINT
The burgers can be individually wrapped in plastic and refrigerated for up to 2 days, or frozen for up to 10 days.

Season the outside of the burgers to taste with salt and pepper and grill over the hot spot to the desired doneness, 4 to 5 minutes per side for medium-rare. As with grilling steaks, if the grill flares up, move the burgers to a cooler spot on the grill and return them to the hot spot when the flare-up subsides.

BONUS POINTS
To make a "regular" all-American hamburger, use only ground beef (with a 20 to 25 percent fat content) and season the outside of the burger to taste with salt and pepper. Follow the above shaping and cooking instructions, resisting the urge to overwork or squeeze the burger, letting it hold together loosely. It'll cook better and the tasty juices will distribute more evenly.

To make your own pickled vegetables to go with burgers or other sandwiches, try this recipe:

PICKLED VEGETABLE SKEWERS

MAKES 8 SKEWERS

1/2 CUPS DISTILLED WHITE VINEGAR

1/4 CUP PACKED LIGHT BROWN SUGAR

I TABLESPOON FENNEL SEEDS

I TEASPOON CRACKED ALLSPICE

3 GARLIC CLOVES, SMASHED AND PEELED

4 FRESH THYME SPRIGS

KOSHER SALT

2 CINNAMON STICKS

I LARGE CUCUMBER, CUT CROSSWISE INTO EIGHT TO TEN 3/4-INCH SLICES

I RED BELL PEPPER, CUT INTO 8 PIECES

8 RED RADISHES

8 SHALLOTS

8 BAMBOO SKEWERS, 8 INCHES LONG, OPTIONAL

In a medium stainless-steel pot, combine the vinegar, sugar, fennel seeds, allspice, garlic, thyme, 2 1/2 tablespoons salt, and cinnamon with 1 1/2 cups water. Bring to a boil over high heat, then reduce to a simmer. Add the cucumber, bell pepper, radishes, and shallots and let simmer for 15 minutes. Remove the pot from the heat and let the pickles cool to room temperature, 50 to 60 minutes. Cover the pot and refrigerate until cold.

BREAK POINT
The vegetables can be refrigerated for 3 to 4 days.

To serve, put 1 piece of each vegetable on each skewer. If serving with the burgers, put 2 skewers in each burger, or simply drain the vegetables and serve them from a bowl.

BEEF TENDERLOIN KEBOBS
WITH **SUMMER VEGETABLES**

SERVES 4

This dish is a celebration of early summer with a mix of vegetables you'll find only at that time of year. If you can't find them, substitute other varieties of onions, squash, or zucchini and cut them down to size. The wine adds a pleasing tart background to the mixture and keeps the dish light and fresh.

Be sure to make the vegetables first so you can serve the dish as soon as the skewers come off the grill.

Serve this with Roasted Garlic Mashed Potatoes (page 162).

FOUR 8-INCH SKEWERS

2 TABLESPOONS CHOPPED FRESH ROSEMARY LEAVES

I TABLESPOON CHOPPED FRESH THYME LEAVES

2 TEASPOONS PULVERIZED GARLIC (SEE PAGE 2I)

2 TABLESPOONS CORN OIL OR OTHER NEUTRAL OIL SUCH AS GRAPESEED OR CANOLA

KOSHER SALT

CRACKED BLACK PEPPER

2 POUNDS BEEF TENDERLOIN TIPS, CUT INTO I2 PIECES

SUMMER VEGETABLES (RECIPE FOLLOWS)

If using bamboo skewers, soak four 8-inch skewers in cold water for 2 to 3 hours before starting.

Stir together the rosemary, thyme, garlic, oil, 2 teaspoons salt, and 1 teaspoon pepper in a small bowl until well incorporated. Add the tenderloin pieces and marinate for 20 to 30 minutes.

Prepare your grill for grilling (see pages 96–100) or use a cast-iron pan.

Put 3 pieces of the beef on each skewer and grill over high heat for 6 to 7 minutes for medium-rare; to check doneness, separate the pieces on the skewer and look at the sides of each piece.

To serve, put the vegetables in a shallow serving bowl with some of their liquid and arrange the skewers on top.

SUMMER VEGETABLES

SERVES 4 AS A SIDE DISH

2 TABLESPOONS CORN OIL OR OTHER NEUTRAL OIL SUCH AS GRAPESEED OR CANOLA

4 CIPOLLINI ONIONS OR PEARL ONIONS, QUARTERED

4 RAMPS, STEMS SEPARATED AND CUT INTO 1½-INCH LENGTHS, LEAVES CUT INTO ¼-INCH JULIENNE

10 OUNCES BABY ZUCCHINI (ABOUT 12), HALVED LENGTHWISE, THEN SLICED INTO ½-INCH PIECES

8 OUNCES PATTYPAN SQUASH (ABOUT 10), QUARTERED

3 OUNCES MOREL MUSHROOMS (ABOUT 16 MUSHROOMS), WELL WASHED AND QUARTERED

4 OUNCES OYSTER MUSHROOMS (ABOUT 2 SMALL CLUSTERS), SEPARATED AND WASHED

¼ CUP DRY WHITE WINE, PREFERABLY CHARDONNAY

1 CUP BEEF STOCK (PAGE 14) OR LOW-SODIUM, STORE-BOUGHT BEEF BROTH

1 TABLESPOON UNSALTED BUTTER

KOSHER SALT

FRESHLY GROUND BLACK PEPPER

TO DRINK
LIGHT/FLORAL WHITE

Heat the oil in a heavy-bottomed sauté pan set over high heat. Add the cipollini onions and ramp stems and cook over high heat until lightly browned, 1 to 2 minutes. Add the zucchini and squash pieces and cook for 2 to 3 minutes. Add morel mushrooms, oyster mushrooms, and ramp leaves and cook for another 2 to 3 minutes.

Pour in the wine, bring to a simmer, and continue to simmer until reduced by half, 1 to 2 minutes. Pour in the stock, bring to a simmer, and continue to simmer until slightly thickened and flavorful, 10 to 12 minutes.

Whisk the butter into the cooking liquid and season with the 2 teaspoons salt and ½ teaspoon pepper.

MARINATED
SKIRT STEAK

SERVES 8

In this recipe, a long marinating time allows many powerful ingredients to penetrate the skirt steak: the acid in balsamic vinegar and Worcestershire sauce doesn't just flavor the meat; it also breaks down connective tissues, making the meat tender.

Serve this with Tabbouleh Salad with Lemon and Cucumber (page 147) or Stewed Tomatoes (page 153).

¾ CUP BALSAMIC VINEGAR

½ CUP CORN OIL OR OTHER NEUTRAL OIL SUCH AS GRAPESEED OR CANOLA

¼ CUP WORCESTERSHIRE SAUCE

2 SHALLOTS, ROUGHLY CHOPPED

2 GARLIC CLOVES

I TABLESPOON CAYENNE PEPPER

I TABLESPOON CHOPPED FRESH CILANTRO LEAVES

I TEASPOON FRESHLY GROUND BLACK PEPPER

I TABLESPOON KOSHER SALT

4 POUNDS SKIRT STEAK, CLEANED OF ALL EXTERIOR FAT AND CONNECTIVE TISSUE

TO DRINK
SPICY RED

Put all the ingredients except the steak in a blender and blend until smooth.

Pour the marinade over the skirt steak in a nonreactive pan.

BREAK POINT
Marinate, refrigerated, for 3 to 4 hours before grilling, but no more than 10 hours.

When ready to cook the steaks, prepare your grill for grilling (see pages 96–100).

Remove the skirt steak from the marinade and clean away any excess marinade with the back of a knife.

Grill the steak over medium-high heat for 4 to 5 minutes per side to serve it rare to medium-rare.

When cooked, slice the steak thinly against the grain, starting at one corner and cutting on the bias. Serve either hot or at room temperature.

STEAKS

If you own this book, chances are you love a great steak. So do I. Here's what you need to know to cook them just the way I do in my restaurants, and at home.

A steak's potential is determined before you set your hands on it. The quality of the beef itself is paramount. So it pays (literally) to make an informed decision at the market.

Generally speaking, I prefer prime-grade, dry-aged beef. As its name suggests, prime is simply the best available. I like mine dry-aged, which results in a nuttier, earthier quality produced by coaxing the excess moisture from the beef to concentrate its texture and flavor.

When shopping for steak in person (as opposed to online), try to get a steak from one of the Big Two breeds—Black Angus and Hereford. Select red meat that looks freshly cut, with bright red edges and white exterior fat. Look for good "marbling," the fat that is naturally grained throughout the steak. As the steak cooks, this fat renders and naturally tenderizes the steak, building in flavor. The steak should not have any undesirable odors. It should smell fresh.

Here's how to buy from various sources: In a perfect world, everyone would have a local butcher shop to draw on, where you can waltz in and tell the guy exactly what you want, and even what you're going to do with it, if that's important to how thick or thin the meat will be cut, whether it will be boned, and so on. A good butcher is the ultimate source for meat, adding one more level of control to your cooking. Moreover,

there's nothing like understanding how to "talk shop" with your butcher to give you a sense of mastery over the entire process. If you have access to such a person, develop that relationship. For the recipes in this book, just walk in and tell him or her what you need. Beyond the world of steaks, butchers can be indispensable for learning about the various cuts of meat, offering advice on how to cook them, or suggesting good substitutions for cuts they might not have on hand.

Believe it or not, when I'm cooking at home, I don't sneak the meat out of one of my restaurant kitchens; I buy it from the local Food Town. Many supermarkets cut the prewrapped steaks in their refrigerated sections too thin, usually ½ to ¾ inch thick. You can't get a char without overcooking the interior. Even in a supermarket, you should feel comfortable asking the butcher to cut steaks to the dimensions mentioned in the recipes. If they're not happy to do it for you, find a new supermarket. And if your supermarket doesn't have a butcher on the premises, try to find one that does. If that's not possible, try mail order. It's fine for mail-order beef to be shipped slightly frozen, which ensures a greater shelf life and guarantees you it hasn't gone without refrigeration during the shipping process. Overnight delivery is crucial. See page 207 for my favorite mail-order beef companies.

GRILLING STEAK

I have a number of strongly held beliefs about how to grill the best steak. The most surprising one might be that I always use oil, salt, and pepper and never opt for more flavorful rubs or marinades. Why? Because steaks cost upward of $16 to $20 per pound, so you want to taste the meat, not use it as a vehicle for other favors that you can enjoy anytime you like for far less money.

Another reason I always stick to oil, salt, and pepper is that they are all you need to get that char that everyone loves.

Just before grilling, shape steaks by gently pressing them in toward the center. This will give you more height, so more control over doneness. Season the steaks with so much salt and pepper that they appear to be overseasoned. There's no set amount for how much salt and pepper, because every cut varies a bit in size from other cuts, but a good rule of thumb is:

- Filet: 1 teaspoon kosher salt, ½ teaspoon coarsely ground black pepper
- Strip: 2½ teaspoons kosher salt, 1 teaspoon coarsely ground black pepper
- Rib eye and porterhouse: 1 tablespoon kosher salt, 1 teaspoon coarsely ground black pepper

For double-cut steaks, do not double the quantities; rather, increase them by 50 percent.

After seasoning, dredge the steaks in oil. It's virtually impossible to overseason a steak headed for the grill. Some of the seasoning comes off in the oil, some on the grill, and the rest turns into that beautiful seared crust, so always err on the side of more salt and pepper.

Set the seasoned steaks on the hot spot of the grill. To get a charred exterior, leave steaks on an uncovered grill for the first 4 to 5 minutes. After this time, cover the grill, but don't go away; the grill will get very hot and the steaks may burn and overcook in the blink of an eye. Monitor the steaks every minute or two, lifting the cover, picking up the steaks with tongs, and examining how much char they are getting. (You can regulate the amount of char depending on your taste. If you like your steak rare to medium-rare and you have 1¼-inch-thick, or thicker, steaks, then more char is a welcome flavor in proportion to the amount of rare meat on the inside.)

When you have the desired char on the first side of the steak, turn the steak over. This is where very careful monitoring is essential; you may or may not have enough time to get the exact same amount of char on the second side.

Telling when a steak is done is not an exact science. Professionals use the so-called "hand" method, which refers to various points on one's hand as a reference point for degrees of doneness. The firm center of your palm corresponds to well-done; the fleshier part at the base of your thumb is rare. This takes practice. It's best to go with an instant-read thermometer: 110° to 115°F is rare; 120°F is medium-rare; 125° to 130°F is medium; 130° to 135°F is medium-well;

and 140°F is well-done. (Take the steaks off the grill when they're 5 to 10 degrees from the target, as they'll continue to cook as they rest. And remember, you can always throw them back on for a minute or two.)

If you have to, there's nothing wrong with cutting a small slit into the meat and examining its color to determine doneness.

In a restaurant kitchen, we refer to one other stage of doneness as black and blue. This refers to a steak that's well charred on the outside but still relatively cool and very rare in the center. If this is how you like your steak, take it off the grill at 95°F.

When steaks are being cooked, the meat contracts and the blood runs to the center of the steak. The steaks need time to rest before serving, 4 to 5 minutes to allow the blood to come back to the edges of the meat and for the tissue to expand.

If cooking indoors on cast iron, you may finish cooking the steak in the oven. See page 100 for more on this.

The following recipes include my guidelines for purchasing and cooking the most popular steak cuts.

NEW YORK STRIP STEAK

This is the cut most Americans picture when they think "steak," a well-marbled block of rich red meat. Seek out center-cut steaks.

The perfect size for a New York strip steak is 1¾ to 2 inches thick with a weight of 14 ounces to 1 pound. The top layer of fat on the steak should be no more than ⅛ inch thick. Avoid vein steaks, the ones with the half-moon-shaped vein running through them; they're too tough.

When grilling, turn a New York strip steak just once, cooking each side for 6 minutes for medium-rare.

RIB CHOP

This steak cut is a bit more difficult to cook due to the quantity of fat, both on the outside and running through the meat. This all but guarantees flare-ups, so don't leave the steak unattended on the grill; it can catch on fire and burn in a matter of seconds.

The perfect size for a rib chop is 2 to 2 ¼ inches thick with a weight of 1 ½ to 2 pounds.

Cook the rib chop until you achieve the desired char on the first side, approximately 10 minutes, moving it when necessary to avoid flare-ups. Turn it over and reduce the heat to medium if using a gas grill, or move the meat over indirect heat on a charcoal grill. Close the lid and cook for approximately 14 more minutes for medium-rare.

RIB CHOP FLORENTINE

SERVES 2

A traditional Tuscan recipe, rib chop Florentine is a preparation using the same steak as above, but it is served sliced with extra virgin olive oil, caramelized garlic, and fresh rosemary.

½ CUP EXTRA VIRGIN OLIVE OIL

4 GARLIC CLOVES, THINLY SLICED

4 FRESH ROSEMARY SPRIGS, ROUGHLY PICKED OF SOME LEAVES (RESERVE A SPRIG WITH SOME LEAVES LEFT ON FOR GARNISH)

2-POUND RIB CHOP, 2 TO 2¼ INCHES THICK

KOSHER SALT

FRESHLY GROUND BLACK PEPPER

To make the oil, heat a small saucepan over high heat and add the olive oil. When the oil is hot, add the garlic and cook until browned, stirring to keep the slices from sticking together. When the garlic is golden brown, add the rosemary leaves. Remove the pan from the heat and stir the oil with a small spoon.

Cook the steak as you would above and when ready remove from the grill. Using a clean cutting board, cut the bone away from the steak and continue to slice the steak into 6 large slices. Arrange the slices on a platter, reheat the oil, and spoon the oil over the steak. Garnish with the rosemary and serve immediately.

FILET MIGNON

The leanest and most tender cut, filet mignon doesn't offer big, beefy flavor, but makes up for it with its buttery texture.

The ideal size for filet mignon is about 12 ounces, center-cut, with no external fat.

Cook a filet as you would a New York strip (page 124). Before grilling, form the filet to stand as tall as possible to ensure even cooking and an attractive shape. Get a good char on the first side, then turn it over and finish cooking.

PORTERHOUSE

A portherhouse includes both sirloin and filet, the best of both worlds, so to speak. A good single-serving cut is about 1¼ inches thick with a weight of about 20 ounces. Cooking it can be a little tricky because the filet side will cook much more quickly than the sirloin side. Just get great char on the first side, flip it, and check the temperature for your desired doneness. (About 6 minutes per side is a pretty good guideline for rare to medium-rare.) I suggest taking a porterhouse off the grill at an internal temperature of about 110°F.

Also worth seeking out is the double porterhouse, which is a porterhouse that's twice as thick as a normal steak, 2½ to 3 inches. That thickness really lets you develop a deep char before the meat has finished cooking within. After charring both sides of a double porterhouse, transfer the meat to a cutting board and cut the filet from the steak. Return the sirloin to the grill and cook to the desired doneness, returning the filet to the grill for the last minute of cooking just to warm it through.

IN THE KITCHEN

These recipes produce my favorite steakhouse-style main-course dishes for the home kitchen.

I've included everything from salmon to turkey to lamb to veal. The beef dish here is short ribs, an inexpensive cut that benefits from the tenderizing effect of slow cooking. Where many of the grilled main courses depend on rubs and marinades for their flavor, this dish and others in this chapter take advantage of the benefits of indoor cooking with techniques like braising that can only be performed in the oven.

Many of the dishes that follow, though designed to be cooked indoors, can also be prepared on the grill. Where this is possible, I've noted it in the recipe instructions.

BAKED LEMON SOLE FILLETS
WITH **CRABMEAT STUFFING** AND **FRESH CORN SAUCE**

SERVES 4

My predisposition toward packing a lot of flavors onto the same plate gets put to the main-course test in this baked fish dish. In many ways, the recipe borrows a page from the crab-cake playbook, with ingredients like Old Bay seasoning, onions, and bread crumbs added to the crab to make a stuffing for the lemon sole. Broiling the fish causes the sauce to take on a unique, soufflé-like texture.

Serve this with Vegetable-Stuffed Ripe Red Tomatoes (page 152).

I TABLESPOON MAYONNAISE

I TEASPOON DIJON MUSTARD

I TABLESPOON CHOPPED FRESH FLAT-LEAF PARSLEY LEAVES

½ TEASPOON CHOPPED FRESH THYME LEAVES PLUS LEAVES FROM 2 THYME SPRIGS

I TEASPOON OLD BAY SEASONING

I LARGE EGG, BEATEN

½ POUND LUMP CRABMEAT, PICKED FREE OF SHELL FRAGMENTS

2 TABLESPOONS DRIED BREAD CRUMBS

4 BONELESS LEMON SOLE FILLETS, 5 OUNCES EACH

2 TABLESPOONS CORN OIL OR OTHER NEUTRAL OIL SUCH AS GRAPESEED OR CANOLA

½ CUP ROUGHLY CHOPPED WHITE ONIONS

2 TEASPOONS MINCED GARLIC

3 CUPS CORN KERNELS, FRESH OR FROZEN

I TABLESPOON SEEDED, MINCED JALAPEÑO

2 TABLESPOONS MINCED FRESH BASIL LEAVES

KOSHER SALT

FRESHLY GROUND BLACK PEPPER

Whisk together the mayonnaise, mustard, parsley, chopped thyme, Old Bay, and egg in a bowl. Gently fold in the crab and bread crumbs. Cover and refrigerate for 15 minutes.

Position a baking rack 8 inches below the broiler and preheat the broiler. If you don't have a broiler deep enough to allow you to position the rack 8 inches from the heat source, preheat the oven to 500°F. Refrigerate until needed.

Lay the sole fillets on a flat surface with the skin side up. Evenly spread about 3 tablespoons of the crab mixture on each fillet. Roll the fillets up around the crab mixture and set on a plate with the seam side down.

To make the corn sauce, heat the oil in a heavy-bottomed saucepan over high heat. Add the onions and garlic and sauté until lightly browned, 1 to 2 minutes. Add the corn and cook, stirring, for 5 minutes. Add the jalapeño, basil, 2 teaspoons salt, ½ teaspoon pepper, and ¾ cup water. Bring to a boil, then reduce the heat and simmer for 6 minutes. Carefully transfer to a blender and blend just until smooth.

Put the corn sauce in the bottom of a 1-quart baking dish to a depth of ½ inch. Put the rolled fish portions in the sauce, seam side down in a single layer. Spread the softened butter on top of each rolled fish portion and sprinkle with the thyme leaves. Add more sauce to the dish until it comes halfway up the sides of the fish.

2 TABLESPOONS UNSALTED BUTTER, SOFTENED AT ROOM TEMPERATURE

TO DRINK
OAKY/FULL-BODIED WHITE
LIGHT/FLORAL WHITE
SPICY RED
AMBER BEER

Put the baking dish in the oven and cook until the sauce begins to set up, approximately 25 minutes. Remove from the oven and let cool for 5 minutes before dividing the fillets among individual plates and serving.

JUMBO SEA SCALLOPS
WITH **WHITE TRUFFLE VINAIGRETTE**

SERVES 4

The white truffle vinaigrette in this dish is highly aromatic and balanced with lemon juice, shallots, and cracked black pepper. I designed it especially to complement the voluptuous texture and uniquely rich flavor of sea scallops, which are meaty enough to take on those flavors without losing their own identity.

The scallops can also be cooked on the grill; make sure it's very clean and well seasoned, and use your fingers to gently squeeze the scallops into as tall a shape as possible before grilling.

3 TABLESPOONS CORN OIL OR OTHER NEUTRAL OIL SUCH AS GRAPESEED OR CANOLA

16 JUMBO SEA SCALLOPS, ABOUT 1½ POUNDS, PREFERABLY DRY-PACKED

KOSHER SALT

FRESHLY GROUND BLACK PEPPER

WHITE TRUFFLE VINAIGRETTE (RECIPE FOLLOWS)

TO DRINK
AROMATIC WHITE

Heat the oil in a nonstick sauté pan over high heat. Season the scallops with 1 tablespoon salt and 2 teaspoons pepper on both sides and put in the pan in batches, taking care not to crowd them. Cook until golden brown on both sides, approximately 2 minutes on each side.

As they are done, arrange 4 scallops on each of 4 dinner plates and drizzle a small amount of the vinaigrette over and around the scallops.

WHITE TRUFFLE VINAIGRETTE

MAKES ABOUT ½ CUP

¼ CUP FINELY DICED SHALLOTS

¼ CUP EXTRA VIRGIN OLIVE OIL

¼ CUP WHITE TRUFFLE OIL

GRATED ZEST AND JUICE OF 3 LEMONS

1½ TEASPOONS KOSHER SALT

¾ TEASPOON CRACKED BLACK PEPPER

¼ CUP MINCED FRESH CHIVES

Mix all of the ingredients except the chives together in a small bowl.

BREAK POINT
The vinaigrette can be covered and refrigerated for up to 2 hours before serving.

Stir in the chives and serve.

TERIYAKI SALMON

SERVES 4

I don't often cook Asian-style food, but the sweet and salty flavors of teriyaki fit my taste sensibility to a T, and I love the way they come together and coat the fish in this dish. You can also make this with other fatty fish such as black cod and halibut, but leave off the skin and cook them for slightly less time.

This can also be cooked on the grill.

Serve this with Summertime Vegetable Packet (page 150).

½ CUP SOY SAUCE

I TABLESPOON SESAME OIL

I TABLESPOON PULVERIZED GARLIC
(SEE PAGE 21)

2 TABLESPOONS PEELED, FINELY
CHOPPED FRESH GINGER

I TEASPOON CAYENNE PEPPER

I TABLESPOON FINELY GRATED LEMON
ZEST

I TABLESPOON FRESHLY SQUEEZED
LEMON JUICE

2 TABLESPOONS LIGHT BROWN SUGAR

¾ CUP EXTRA VIRGIN OLIVE OIL

¼ CUP FINELY CHOPPED FRESH
CILANTRO LEAVES

4 BONELESS SALMON FILLETS, SKIN
ON, ABOUT 7 OUNCES EACH

2 TABLESPOONS CORN OIL OR OTHER
NEUTRAL OIL SUCH AS GRAPESEED
OR CANOLA

TO DRINK
LIGHT/FLORAL WHITE
BLOND BEER

Mix the soy sauce, sesame oil, garlic, ginger, cayenne, lemon zest and juice, sugar, olive oil, and cilantro in a small bowl. Put the salmon fillets in a single layer in a baking dish or other shallow vessel. Pour the marinade over the salmon. Cover and marinate for 20 to 30 minutes.

Heat the corn oil in a nonstick pan over high heat. Remove the salmon from the marinade and let the marinade run off. Pat dry with paper towels.

Put the fish skin side down in the hot pan. Cook until the skin is crisp, 5 to 6 minutes. Lower the heat, turn the salmon over, and continue to cook for an additional 3 to 4 minutes.

Transfer 1 fillet to each of 4 dinner plates and serve.

CORIANDER-BRAISED CHICKEN
WITH **STEAMED SPINACH**

SERVES 6

If one-pot dishes are your thing, make this chicken. The sauce reduces to a pleasant, nappy consistency punched up with orange and coriander, almost like chicken à l'orange. The spinach is what takes this to the level of a meal in its own right, putting six servings' worth of the vegetable right in the pot with the chicken and sauce.

2 CHICKENS, 3 POUNDS EACH, QUARTERED

KOSHER SALT

FRESHLY GROUND BLACK PEPPER

3 TABLESPOONS CORN OIL OR OTHER NEUTRAL OIL SUCH AS GRAPESEED OR CANOLA

3 CELERY STALKS, ROUGHLY CHOPPED

½ WHITE ONION, ROUGHLY CHOPPED

4 GARLIC CLOVES, THINLY SLICED

PEEL OF I ORANGE, REMOVED IN STRIPS WITH A VEGETABLE PEELER

½ CUP CRACKED CORIANDER SEEDS

¼ CUP GRAND MARNIER

2 CUPS ORANGE JUICE

6 CUPS CHICKEN STOCK (PAGE 13) OR LOW-SODIUM, STORE-BOUGHT CHICKEN BROTH

¼ CUP ROUGHLY CHOPPED FRESH CILANTRO LEAVES

2 PACKAGES FRESH SPINACH, IO OUNCES EACH

TO DRINK
OAKY/FULL-BODIED WHITE
AMBER BEER
RICH/DARK BEER

Preheat the oven to 375°F.

Season the chickens with 1 teaspoon salt and ½ teaspoon pepper.

Set a roasting pan on the stovetop, add the oil, and heat over medium heat. Add the celery, onion, garlic, and orange peel and cook until the onion is translucent, 6 to 7 minutes.

Add the coriander and toast until fragrant, 2 to 3 minutes. Add the Grand Marnier, allow to heat for a moment, and either light with a match or tip the pan gently toward the burner flame to ignite and cook off the alcohol. (If you're uncomfortable flambéing, set the pan on a trivet or pot holder, ignite a match, stand back, and ignite the alcohol. After it burns off, you can return the pan to the heat.)

Add the orange juice, chicken stock, cilantro, 1 tablespoon salt, and 1 teaspoon pepper. Bring to a boil, then reduce to a simmer. Let simmer until reduced by one-third, 12 to 15 minutes. Add the chicken pieces. Place in the oven, uncovered, and cook for 1 hour, basting occasionally. Remove the breast pieces and cook the legs for an additional 30 minutes.

When ready, remove the legs and strain the sauce through a fine-mesh strainer into a pot. Bring the sauce to a boil and add the spinach a handful at a time, cooking each batch until wilted and tender, 3 to 4 minutes, before adding the next handful. Return all of the chicken to the pan and cook for 5 minutes.

To serve, use tongs to transfer the spinach to a deep serving tray and surround with the chicken pieces. Pass the sauce alongside in a sauceboat.

BACON-WRAPPED TURKEY
WITH **GREEN CHILE–ALMOND SAUCE**

SERVES 4 (MAKES 8 PIECES, 5 OUNCES EACH)

Guess what: turkey doesn't get along just with bread stuffing, gravy, and cranberry sauce. Here, the mellow heat of green chiles proves to be a perfectly logical accompaniment as well. To infuse the turkey itself with as much flavor as possible, it's rubbed with a paste of roasted garlic, thyme, and lemon zest, then wrapped in bacon.

This dish is also delicious prepared on the grill; be prepared to move the pieces around if the bacon drippings cause flare-ups.

Serve this with Toasted Barley Risotto with Mushrooms and Thyme (page 167).

¼ CUP PUREED ROASTED GARLIC (PAGE 15)

2 TEASPOONS MINCED FRESH THYME LEAVES

2 TEASPOONS FINELY GRATED LEMON ZEST

2 TABLESPOONS PLUS 2 TEASPOONS CORN OIL OR OTHER NEUTRAL OIL SUCH AS GRAPESEED OR CANOLA

KOSHER SALT

FRESHLY GROUND BLACK PEPPER

3 POUNDS SKINLESS, BONELESS TURKEY BREAST, CUT INTO SAUSAGE-LIKE PIECES APPROXIMATELY 1½ BY 1½ BY 6 INCHES

1½ POUNDS SLAB BACON, THINLY SLICED (ABOUT 24 SLICES)

GREEN CHILE–ALMOND SAUCE (RECIPE FOLLOWS)

Preheat the oven to 400°F.

Mix the garlic puree, thyme, lemon zest, 2 tablespoons oil, ¾ teaspoon salt, and ½ teaspoon pepper into a paste. Coat the turkey portions with this mixture. Lay out 3 or 4 slices of bacon, edges overlapping slightly. Place a piece of turkey on the bacon and roll the bacon around the turkey. Repeat with the remaining bacon and turkey. Place on a plate with the seam side down until ready to cook.

Heat the 2 teaspoons oil in a large, ovenproof sauté pan. Put the turkey rolls seam side down in the hot pan and brown on all sides, about 10 minutes. Transfer the pan to the oven and roast until the bacon is crisp and an instant-read thermometer inserted in the thickest part of the roll reads 165°F, 12 to 14 minutes.

To serve, slice the turkey on the bias into ½- to ¾-inch pieces and arrange the pieces on a platter. Pass the sauce alongside in a sauceboat.

(CONTINUED)

GREEN CHILE–ALMOND SAUCE

MAKES 3 CUPS

¾ CUP SLICED ALMONDS

2 TABLESPOONS CORN OIL OR OTHER
NEUTRAL OIL SUCH AS GRAPESEED
OR CANOLA

4 ANAHEIM CHILES, STEMMED
AND SEEDED

⅓ CUP ROUGHLY CHOPPED WHITE
ONION

1 TABLESPOON ROUGHLY CHOPPED
GARLIC

2 CUPS LOW-SODIUM, STORE-BOUGHT
VEGETABLE BROTH OR WATER

KOSHER SALT

½ CUP CHOPPED FRESH CILANTRO
LEAVES

1 TABLESPOON FRESHLY SQUEEZED
LIME JUICE

TO DRINK
SMOOTH/MEDIUM-BODIED RED
AMBER BEER

Preheat the oven to 300°F. Spread the almonds out on a baking sheet and toast until dark golden brown, approximately 5 minutes.

In a large, heavy-bottomed saucepan, heat the oil over medium-high heat. Add the chiles, onion, and garlic and cook until softened and lightly browned, approximately 4 minutes. Add the almonds, broth, and 2½ teaspoons salt. Simmer until slightly thickened, approximately 10 minutes. Remove the pan from the heat and add the cilantro. Place the sauce in a blender and puree until smooth. Before serving, add the fresh lime juice.

The sauce can be covered and refrigerated for up to 6 hours.

Smoked Chile Burger (page 116) with
Garlic-Herb French Fries (page 160) and Berry Lemonade (page 31)

Beef Tenderloin Kebobs with Summer Vegetables (page 118)

New York Strip Steak (page 124),
Black Truffle Creamed Spinach (page 154), and Gruyère Potato Gratin (page 166)

Rib Chop Florentine (page 125)

Baked Lemon Sole Fillets Stuffed with Crabmeat and Fresh Corn Sauce (page 128)

Jumbo Sea Scallops with White Truffle Vinaigrette (page 130)

Teriyaki Salmon (page 131) with Summertime Vegetable Packet (page 150)

Creamy Mascarpone Cheesecake with Marinated Fresh Raspberries (page 198)

VEAL BREAST
WITH **BASIL** AND **FENNEL SEED PESTO** AND **STEWED VEGETABLES**

SERVES 6

Veal breast has the ability to take on other flavors very successfully. Here, it's flavored from within and without: a basil and fennel seed mixture is pureed and spread over the veal, which is then rolled, tied, and braised. The meat becomes very soft and absorbs the qualities of the herb mixture, as well as the aromatics in the braising liquid. When you slice the roast into pieces, a nice presentation naturally occurs as the meat frames the filling in each slice. Serve this with Chive Mashed Potatoes (page 162).

I CUP LIGHTLY PACKED FRESH BASIL LEAVES

2 TABLESPOONS SLICED GARLIC (FROM ABOUT 3 CLOVES)

I TABLESPOON FINELY GRATED LEMON ZEST

2 TEASPOONS GROUND FENNEL SEEDS

KOSHER SALT

FRESHLY GROUND BLACK PEPPER

¾ CUP CORN OIL OR OTHER NEUTRAL OIL SUCH AS GRAPESEED OR CANOLA

5 POUNDS BONED VEAL BREAST, IN I PIECE

2 CARROTS, HALVED LENGTHWISE AND CUT INTO 4-INCH SEGMENTS

3 CELERY STALKS, CUT CROSSWISE INTO THIRDS

I WHITE ONION, CUT INTO 6 WEDGES

2 CUPS DRY WHITE WINE

3 BAY LEAVES

4 FRESH THYME SPRIGS

2 FRESH ROSEMARY SPRIGS

I CUP LOW-SODIUM, STORE-BOUGHT BEEF BROTH

TO DRINK
OAKY/FULL-BODIED WHITE

Preheat the oven to 375°F.

Place the basil, garlic, lemon zest, fennel seeds, 1 tablespoon salt, 2 teaspoons black pepper, and ½ cup of the oil in a blender and gently pack down with a rubber spatula. Puree until smooth, about 30 seconds. Turn off the blender and pack down toward the blade, if needed, to get everything smooth.

Lay the veal breast on a flat surface. Spread the basil pesto to coat the inside of the veal breast. Roll up the veal so the pesto is in the center of the roulade. Using butcher twine, tie the veal roulade every 1½ inches until the whole piece is tied.

Season the veal with 1 tablespoon salt and 2 teaspoons pepper. Heat 2 tablespoons of the oil in a sauté pan large enough to accommodate the veal and brown the outside evenly, 3 to 4 minutes per side.

In a large, heavy-bottomed Dutch oven or roasting pan, heat the remaining 2 tablespoons oil. Add the carrots, celery, and onion and sauté until softened but not browned, approximately 8 minutes. Season with 1½ tablespoons salt and 1 tablespoon pepper. Pour in the wine and add the bay leaves, thyme, and rosemary. Cook over medium-high heat until the wine is slightly reduced, 5 to 6 minutes. Pour in the beef broth and bring to a boil. Reduce the heat to a simmer and add the tied veal breast. Braise in the oven for 3 hours. The sauce will thicken and reduce.

To serve, remove the veal from the Dutch oven. Cut the twine off the veal and slice into 2-inch slices. Serve with the vegetables and sauce.

BLACKENED VEAL MEDALLIONS

WITH **PARSLEY–RED PEPPER SALAD**

SERVES 4

Veal medallions, coated in a spicy Cajun dry rub and blackened in a cast-iron pan, would be delicious on their own. But when you add an acidic, herbaceous salad of roasted red peppers and parsley to relieve the heat of the spices, it becomes more compelling and complex and allows each person to alternate bites of hot and cold sensations.

The lesson here is that when using a dry rub, you want the meat to be relatively thin so the spices don't burn in the time it takes to cook the meat.

Serve this with Roasted Garlic Mashed Potatoes (page 162).

2½ POUNDS VEAL TENDERLOIN, CUT INTO 12 PIECES (VEAL EYE ROUND CAN BE SUBSTITUTED) AND POUNDED TO ½-INCH MEDALLIONS

¼ CUP CORN OIL OR OTHER NEUTRAL OIL SUCH AS GRAPESEED OR CANOLA

⅓ CUP SPICE RUB (RECIPE FOLLOWS)

½ CUP ROUGHLY CHOPPED FRESH FLAT-LEAF PARSLEY LEAVES

1 CUP JULIENNED STORE-BOUGHT ROASTED RED BELL PEPPERS

2 CUPS MIXED BABY LETTUCES

KOSHER SALT

FRESHLY GROUND BLACK PEPPER

¼ CUP SHERRY VINAIGRETTE (PAGE 11)

TO DRINK
CRISP/FRESH WHITE
LIGHT-BODIED BEER

Lightly coat the tenderloin pieces with the oil. Spread the spice rub out on a plate. Dredge the veal medallions in the spice rub, pressing down to generously coat them on all sides with the rub. As they are ready, gather them on a plate.

Heat a cast-iron pan on the stovetop and cook the veal medallions for 3 to 4 minutes on each side. Remove from the heat and allow to rest for 3 to 4 minutes.

While the veal is resting, toss the parsley, peppers, lettuces, 1 teaspoon salt, ¼ teaspoon pepper, and vinaigrette together in a bowl.

Serve family style by placing the cooked veal medallions in a large serving dish and garnish with the salad.

SPICE RUB

MAKES ⅓ CUP

This rub is also good on chicken cutlets or meaty fish such as swordfish.

Mix all the ingredients in a small bowl.

I TABLESPOON FRESHLY GROUND BLACK PEPPER

I TABLESPOON KOSHER SALT

I TABLESPOON MINCED FRESH THYME LEAVES

I TEASPOON GROUND CUMIN

I TEASPOON GROUND CORIANDER

I TEASPOON SWEET SPANISH PAPRIKA

I TEASPOON GROUND CINNAMON

I TEASPOON DRY MUSTARD

I TEASPOON GARLIC POWDER

½ TEASPOON CAYENNE PEPPER

CIDER AND STOUT
ROASTED PORK SHOULDER

SERVES 6 TO 8

Brining pork for hours makes cooking it virtually foolproof. Here the pork is slow-cooked in a tenderizing, apple cider–based liquid. The shoulder turns meltingly tender, which also makes for great leftovers and sandwiches the next day.

Use two pieces of pork shoulder—the relatively small diameter allows the brine to penetrate each piece deeply and helps the pork cook more evenly.

Serve this with Glazed Butternut Squash with Maple and Autumn Spices (page 157).

4 CUPS CIDER VINEGAR

I CUP SUGAR

KOSHER SALT

6 BAY LEAVES

II FRESH THYME SPRIGS

¼ CUP CORIANDER SEEDS

4 POUNDS PORK SHOULDER (TWO 2-POUND ROASTS, NETTED OR TIED, ABOUT 8 INCHES LONG AND 4 TO 5 INCHES IN DIAMETER)

¼ CUP VEGETABLE OR CORN OIL OR OTHER NEUTRAL OIL SUCH AS GRAPESEED OR CANOLA

I WHITE ONION, CUT INTO EIGHTHS

4 CELERY STALKS, CUT INTO 4-INCH SEGMENTS

3 CARROTS, HALVED LENGTHWISE AND CUT INTO 4-INCH SEGMENTS

I APPLE, CORED AND QUARTERED

I FENNEL BULB, TRIMMED AND QUARTERED

3 FRESH ROSEMARY SPRIGS

I QUART APPLE CIDER

12-OUNCE BOTTLE STOUT

Pour 6 cups water into a large pot. Add the vinegar, sugar, ½ cup salt, 3 of the bay leaves, 5 of the thyme sprigs, and the coriander. Bring to a boil, then lower the heat and let simmer for 30 minutes. Let cool completely. Add the pork, cover, and refrigerate for 8 to 12 hours (but no longer than 15). If the pork isn't completely submerged, stir in just enough cold water to bring the brine over the top.

When ready to proceed, remove the pork from the brine and wipe off any herbs and spices that may have adhered to it. Discard the brine.

Preheat the oven to 400°F.

Preheat a large roasting pan in the oven for about 10 minutes. Pour in the oil and turn the pan to coat the surface with oil. Add the onion, celery, carrots, apple, fennel, rosemary, remaining 3 bay leaves, and remaining 6 thyme sprigs; stir quickly and roast for 10 to 12 minutes. Add the cider and stout and let cook for 5 to 6 minutes. Add the pork and roast, basting every 10 minutes, for 1 hour, or until the internal temperature is 140°F as measured with an instant-read thermometer.

Remove from the oven and allow to rest for 15 to 20 minutes. The vegetables will be intact and the sauce reduced to a thin consistency when done.

TO DRINK
SPICY RED
AMBER BEER

To serve, slice the pork roast into ½-inch slices and arrange with the vegetables on a serving tray. There's no need to strain the sauce; just remove the vegetables with a slotted spoon and place them around the pork on the tray. Then pour the sauce into a sauceboat and pass alongside.

WHOLE RACK OF LAMB
MARINATED IN ROSEMARY, LEMON, AND GARLIC

SERVES 4

Try this recipe and you'll see for yourself how easy it is to cook and serve elegant rack of lamb at home. The vegetable "raft" is more than a flavoring device; it's also a tangy accompaniment to the meat on the finished plate. If you like, present the rack whole to your guests and slice it into chops at the table.

Serve this with Black Truffle Creamed Spinach (page 154).

2 TABLESPOONS PUREED ROASTED GARLIC (PAGE 15)

¼ CUP CHOPPED FRESH ROSEMARY LEAVES

I TABLESPOON DIJON MUSTARD

2 TABLESPOONS OLIVE OIL

2 TABLESPOONS FRESHLY SQUEEZED LEMON JUICE

KOSHER SALT

FRESHLY GROUND BLACK PEPPER

2 LAMB RACKS, ABOUT 2 POUNDS EACH (8 CHOPS PER RACK)

I TABLESPOON UNSALTED BUTTER

6 CELERY STALKS, CUT INTO 3-INCH SEGMENTS

I FENNEL BULB, TRIMMED AND CUT INTO ¾-INCH SLICES

2 LEMONS, CUT INTO ½-INCH SLICES

I CUP VEGETABLE STOCK (PAGE 12) OR LOW-SODIUM, STORE-BOUGHT VEGETABLE BROTH

TO DRINK
SMOOTH/MEDIUM-BODIED RED

Stir together the garlic, rosemary, mustard, oil, lemon juice, 1 teaspoon salt, and ½ teaspoon pepper into a thick paste in a bowl. Generously rub the paste over the lamb, set the lamb in a baking dish or other shallow vessel, cover loosely with plastic wrap, and let marinate for 30 to 45 minutes.

BREAK POINT
The lamb can marinate for up to 4 hours before cooking. If marinating for more than 45 minutes, refrigerate it and let it come to room temperature for 10 minutes before cooking.

Preheat the oven to 425°F.

Heat a roasting pan in the preheated oven. Add the butter and let it melt. Add the celery, fennel, and lemon slices, arranging them as a "raft" to hold the lamb. Gently pour the stock around the vegetables. Place the lamb racks on top of the vegetables and roast until the internal temperature is 105°F for medium-rare, 30 to 35 minutes, or 120°F for medium-well to well-done. When the desired temperature is reached, remove the pan from the oven, remove the lamb from the pan, and let it rest for 6 to 8 minutes.

BREAK POINT
The lamb can be kept for up to 40 minutes before serving if you stop the initial cooking when the internal temperature reaches 95°F, after about 20 minutes. Reheat the chops in an oven set to 425°F for 6 to 8 minutes just before serving.

To serve, arrange the roasted vegetables on a serving tray. Slice the racks into individual chops and arrange on the tray. Present family style at the table.

LAMB RACK "PRIME RIB"
STUFFED WITH MERGUEZ SAUSAGE

SERVES 4

This flavor-packed recipe let's you take advantage of the shape and structure of lamb racks by stuffing them with a lamb sausage and cheese mixture in a pocket cut along the bones. Those ingredients infuse the meat with spice and tang and also serve to keep it nicely moist, making this a very forgiving dish to prepare.

Serve this with Vegetable-Stuffed Ripe Red Tomatoes (page 152).

2 LAMB RACKS, FAT TRIMMED TO 1/4 INCH THICK, BONES FRENCHED 3 INCHES FROM THE END

10 OUNCES MERGUEZ SAUSAGE, REMOVED FROM CASING

1/2 CUP GOAT CHEESE

1/4 CUP DRIED BREAD CRUMBS

2 TABLESPOONS CORN OIL OR OTHER NEUTRAL OIL SUCH AS GRAPESEED OR CANOLA

3 TABLESPOONS DIJON MUSTARD

TO DRINK
SMOOTH/MEDIUM-BODIED RED
SPICY RED

Cut a pocket along the bones of the lamb racks, starting where the fat meets the bones and cutting toward the eye.

Heat a heavy-bottomed sauté pan over medium-high heat. Crumble the sausage, add to the pan, and cook, stirring, until starting to brown, 5 to 6 minutes. Use tongs or a slotted spoon to transfer the sausage to a bowl, letting any excess fat drain off. Let the sausage cool to room temperature.

Preheat the oven to 400°F.

Crumble the goat cheese into the bowl and stir in the bread crumbs. Divide this mixture among the slits in the lamb racks, packing it in tightly.

Tie the racks closed between each bone with butcher's twine.

Heat the oil in a large, heavy-bottomed sauté pan and brown the exterior of the lamb rack, 7 to 8 minutes. Using a pastry brush, lightly coat the exterior of the lamb with the mustard. Place the rack "cap" side down in the pan and place in the oven.

Roast the lamb rack until the internal temperature is 105°F for medium-rare, 14 to 15 minutes. Remove the lamb rack from the oven and let rest for 3 to 4 minutes before slicing into individual chops and dividing among 4 dinner plates.

ORANGE-BRAISED
LAMB SHANKS

SERVES 4

Lamb shanks are very popular these days because they're easy to cook—you just sear them, make a braising base, and let them simmer away for hours—but intensely flavored. Here, the shanks are cooked in an orange-flavored liquid that is reduced to a glaze and brushed on the shanks. They're really decadent, with a surprise kick from the heat of the red chile flakes. Be sure to reduce the liquid all the way down; you might get down to just a cup or so before it becomes syrupy enough to do the trick.

Serve this with Cheddar Mashed Potatoes (page 162).

¼ CUP CORN OIL OR OTHER NEUTRAL OIL SUCH AS GRAPESEED OR CANOLA

4 LAMB SHANKS, ABOUT 1 POUND EACH

KOSHER SALT

FRESHLY GROUND BLACK PEPPER

1 CUP ROUGHLY CUT ONIONS

1 CUP GARLIC CLOVES

1 CUP ROUGHLY CUT CELERY

¾ CUP ORANGE PEEL, STRIPS REMOVED WITH A VEGETABLE PEELER

½ CUP GRAND MARNIER

4 CUPS ORANGE JUICE

6 CUPS BEEF STOCK (PAGE 14) OR LOW-SODIUM, STORE-BOUGHT BEEF BROTH

1 TABLESPOON CORIANDER SEEDS

2 TEASPOON CRUSHED RED PEPPER FLAKES

1 TABLESPOON LIGHT BROWN SUGAR

TO DRINK
SMOOTH/MEDIUM-BODIED RED
RICH/DARK BEER

Heat 2 tablespoons of the oil in a large sauté pan. Season the shanks to taste with salt and pepper and sauté until browned, approximately 10 minutes.

Heat the remaining 2 tablespoons oil in a large pot or Dutch oven over medium-high heat. Add the onions, garlic, celery, and orange peel and sauté until lightly browned and softened, 6 to 7 minutes. Lean back and add the Grand Marnier. Flame to burn off the alcohol.

Pour in the orange juice and beef stock and add the coriander seeds, pepper flakes, brown sugar, 2 teaspoons salt, and 1 teaspoon pepper. Bring to a boil and add the seared lamb shanks. Reduce the heat until the liquid is simmering and cover. Cook at a simmer for 2½ hours. To test for doneness, pull away the lamb meat with a fork. There should be no resistance. Remove the lamb shanks from the liquid. Strain the liquid and discard the solids. Reduce the liquid to 1 cup.

Coat the lamb shanks with the liquid. Place the lamb on a tray and place under the broiler. Broil for 4 to 5 minutes, turning and glazing with the braising liquid.

To serve, arrange the shanks on a platter and present family style.

BARBECUE-BRAISED
BEEF SHORT RIBS

SERVES 4

What's this barbecue recipe doing in a chapter full of indoor main courses? Look ahead and you'll see that it's not true barbecue; the ribs are cooked entirely indoors. But the super-tangy sauce and the smoky flavor imparted by the chipotle, which is after all a smoked jalapeño, makes these taste very close to what you'd get outdoors. A great recipe to have on call during the colder months of the year. Serve this with Collard Greens (page 156).

¼ CUP CORN OIL OR OTHER NEUTRAL OIL SUCH AS GRAPESEED OR CANOLA

4 POUNDS BEEF SHORT RIBS, CUT INTO INDIVIDUAL RIBS ABOUT 4 INCHES LONG

KOSHER SALT

FRESHLY GROUND BLACK PEPPER

½ CUP FINELY DICED WHITE ONIONS

¼ CUP THINLY SLICED GARLIC (FROM ABOUT 12 CLOVES)

I CUP RED WINE VINEGAR

I TABLESPOON FINELY CHOPPED CANNED CHIPOTLE IN ADOBO

2 CUPS STRONG DECAF COFFEE

2½ CUPS CANNED CRUSHED TOMATOES

¼ CUP PACKED LIGHT BROWN SUGAR

I CUP ORANGE JUICE

¼ CUP FINELY CHOPPED FRESH CILANTRO LEAVES

TO DRINK
LIGHT/FLORAL WHITE
SMOOTH/MEDIUM-BODIED RED
AMBER BEER

Preheat the oven to 375°F.

Heat 2 tablespoons of the oil in a sauté pan. Season the ribs with 2 tablespoons salt and 2 teaspoons pepper. Add the ribs to the pan and brown them for about 10 minutes, until all of the ribs are very brown and well seared.

Heat the remaining 2 tablespoons oil in a heavy-bottomed pot over high heat. Sauté the onions and garlic until lightly browned, 4 to 5 minutes. Add the vinegar, chipotle, and coffee. Cook over medium-high heat until reduced by one-third, 10 to 12 minutes. Add the tomatoes, sugar, orange juice, and cilantro and cook for 20 minutes. Add the ribs. Put the pot in the oven, uncovered, and braise the short ribs for 2 hours or until fork tender.

Remove the pot from the oven. Preheat the broiler.

Pull the short rib meat from the bones and discard the bones. Put the meat in an ovenproof casserole. Degrease the sauce and smother the ribs with the sauce, using it all. Broil until the sauce thickens and begins to cling to the ribs, 8 to 10 minutes.

To serve, divide the ribs among individual plates or serve family style from a platter.

SCENE-STEALING SIDES

I don't think it's possible to become a steakhouse specialist without falling in love with side dishes. The mix-and-match aspect of a steakhouse meal is one of its most appealing characteristics, especially in today's dining environment, where the main course often includes an accompaniment or two plus a sauce, leaving the diner with very little say in the meal.

In steakhouses, you order your meat or fish à la carte, selecting whatever sauces and/or sides you want. With very few exceptions, everyone gets his or her own cut, plus a choice of what to put on the plate with it. It's not unusual for a table to order more than they can eat, simply because they want to taste as many different sides as possible.

My steakhouse menus offer a selection of sides that are largely inspired by traditional steakhouse staples, such as macaroni and cheese, creamed spinach, and potatoes. But we do something different with all of them, so they are both familiar and new at the same time.

Passing sides recalls dining in a home setting, hence the term "family style." So it's quite fitting to maintain the steakhouse menu format in this book because it's how most of us are used to cooking and eating in our own homes.

TABBOULEH SALAD

with **LEMON AND CUCUMBER**

SERVES 4 TO 6

The Middle Eastern salad tabbouleh is a quick and easy lunch or dinner dish of bulgur wheat, vegetables, and mint. The lemon vinaigrette provides a more complex, nuanced dressing than the conventional lemon juice. You can use diced red and/or green bell peppers, either of which adds a pleasing crunch, instead of the cucumber.

1½ CUPS BULGUR WHEAT
(ABOUT 9 OUNCES)

½ CUP DICED RED ONIONS

¾ CUP DICED PLUM TOMATOES
(FROM ABOUT 2 TOMATOES)

¾ CUP DICED PEELED CUCUMBER
(ABOUT HALF A LARGE CUCUMBER)

2½ TEASPOONS KOSHER SALT

½ CUP LEMON VINAIGRETTE (PAGE 11)

1 TEASPOON FINELY GRATED LEMON
ZEST

2 TABLESPOONS CHOPPED FRESH FLAT-
LEAF PARSLEY LEAVES

1 TABLESPOON CHOPPED FRESH MINT
LEAVES

Place the bulgur wheat in a bowl. Bring 1½ cups water to a boil. Pour the boiling water over the bulgur wheat and stir with a fork. Cover the bowl with plastic wrap and let sit in a warm place on the counter for 45 minutes. Fluff the softened bulgur with a fork.

Add the remaining ingredients and toss well with a fork to incorporate them.

Serve the tabbouleh family style from a bowl.

CURRIED PEAS AND CORN

SERVES 4

The addition of curry powder to peas and corn takes the combination to new heights because the contrast offered by the spices brings the distinct sweetness of the peas and corn into high relief, and the vegetables emphasize the spicy edge of the curry. Don't overcook this—you want the vegetables nice and crunchy, and the entire dish should be vibrant to both the eyes and the palate.

2 TABLESPOONS CORN OR VEGETABLE OIL

½ CUP FINELY DICED WHITE ONIONS

I TABLESPOON THINLY SLICED GARLIC

I TABLESPOON CURRY POWDER

½ CUP WHITE WINE (A BRIGHT AND CRISP ONE, SUCH AS SAUVIGNON BLANC)

I CUP HEAVY CREAM

I TEASPOON MINCED FRESH THYME LEAVES

2 CUPS CORN KERNELS, FRESH OR DEFROSTED FROZEN

I CUP FRESH PEAS OR DEFROSTED FROZEN PEAS (PETIT POIS)

I TABLESPOON MINCED FRESH THAI BASIL LEAVES OR 2 TABLESPOONS MINCED SWEET BASIL LEAVES

KOSHER SALT

Heat the oil in a medium pot over high heat. Add the onions and garlic and sauté until softened but not browned, approximately 4 minutes. Add the curry powder and let it toast and become fragrant, 30 to 45 seconds. Pour in the wine, raise the heat to high, and bring it to a boil. Pour in the cream and reduce by one-third, approximately 5 minutes.

Add the thyme and corn, lower the heat to low, and let cook gently until the mixture is slightly thickened.

BREAK POINT
You can cover the mixture and keep it at room temperature for up to 1 hour. Then gently reheat and proceed.

When ready to serve, add the peas, basil, and 1 teaspoon salt and warm through for 1 to 2 minutes, stirring constantly. Serve hot.

SWEET CORN ON THE COB
WITH SUN-DRIED TOMATO BUTTER

SERVES 8

Corn and tomato, the two beloved ingredients of late summer, come together here as never before. By wrapping tomato butter in the corn's husks during grilling, the cobs take on a rich, deep, sweet flavor.

8 EARS CORN

12 SUN-DRIED TOMATOES

½ POUND (2 STICKS) UNSALTED BUTTER, SOFTENED AT ROOM TEMPERATURE

3 GARLIC CLOVES

1 TEASPOON GRATED LEMON ZEST

2 TABLESPOONS JULIENNED FRESH BASIL LEAVES

3 TABLESPOONS CHOPPED FRESH FLAT-LEAF PARSLEY LEAVES

KOSHER SALT

FRESHLY GROUND BLACK PEPPER

Pull the husks away from the corn, leaving them attached at the end. Remove the silk from the corn and re-cover the corn with the husks. Fill a large bowl halfway with cold water. Add the corn to the water, set a heavy plate on top to make sure the ears are immersed, and soak for 1 to 2 hours.

Meanwhile, put the sun-dried tomatoes in a small saucepan and cover with cold water. Bring the water to a boil over high heat, then remove from the heat and let steep for 10 to 15 minutes. Drain the tomatoes in a fine-mesh strainer set over a bowl. Reserve the liquid.

Put the tomatoes in a blender or food processor fitted with the steel blade. Add ½ cup of the steeping liquid and pulse to puree.

Put the softened butter in the bowl of a mixer fitted with the paddle attachment and paddle the butter until smooth. (Or you can whip the butter in a bowl with a wooden spoon until smooth.) Add the pureed sun-dried tomatoes, garlic, lemon zest, basil, and parsley. Season with 1 tablespoon salt and 1 teaspoon pepper.

BREAK POINT
Cover the butter and chill for at least 3 hours. The butter can be refrigerated for up to 3 days, or rolled into a log, wrapped in plastic wrap, and frozen for up to 2 months.

Prepare your grill for grilling (see pages 96–100).

After the corn has been soaked, pull the husks back and generously coat the corn with the sun-dried tomato butter. Cover the corn with the husks and tie with butcher's twine.

(CONTINUED)

VEGETABLE-STUFFED
RIPE RED TOMATOES

SERVES 6

This dish takes the ingredients of ratatouille and stuffs them into a luscious, ripe, red tomato. The sweetness of the tomato and the crunch of the herbed bread crumb topping transform this into another dish altogether.

6 RIPE RED BEEFSTEAK TOMATOES

2½ CUPS TOMATO-ZUCCHINI RELISH (DOUBLE THE RECIPE ON PAGE 44)

¾ CUP BREAD CRUMB TOPPING (PAGE 17)

Preheat the oven to 350°F.

Cut off and discard the top half of each tomato. Using a spoon, remove the flesh and seeds (reserving them) to create a bowl, taking care not to rupture the skin. Chop the tomato flesh and seeds and stir them into the relish. Fill each hollowed tomato with 4 to 5 tablespoons of the tomato-zucchini relish and place them in a baking dish.

Top each stuffed tomato with a generous tablespoon of bread crumbs. Pour ½ cup water into the bottom of the dish and bake until the tomato shell is tender but still holds its shape, 30 to 35 minutes. The filling should be hot throughout, and the bread crumbs should be golden brown and crisp. Check the internal temperature of the filling by inserting a metal skewer or paring knife. The skewer or knife blade should be hot when removed.

Serve the tomatoes alongside other items or from a platter.

STEWED TOMATOES

SERVES 6 TO 8

My version of stewed tomatoes is as much a stew as it is tomatoes, with onions, garlic, carrots, and basil added to the mix. The tomatoes are baked in a casserole with bread crumbs.

3 TABLESPOONS CORN OIL OR OTHER NEUTRAL OIL SUCH AS GRAPESEED OR CANOLA

½ CUP COARSELY GRATED WHITE ONIONS

I TABLESPOON THINLY SLICED GARLIC

2 CUPS COARSELY GRATED CARROTS (FROM ABOUT 2 MEDIUM CARROTS)

¾ CUP SHERRY VINEGAR

5 CUPS WHOLE, PEELED, CANNED PLUM TOMATOES IN JUICE (FROM THREE 15-OUNCE CANS)

I½ TABLESPOONS CHOPPED FRESH BASIL LEAVES

I TEASPOON GRATED LEMON ZEST

KOSHER SALT

FRESHLY GROUND BLACK PEPPER

2 CUPS DICED SOURDOUGH BREAD

BREAD CRUMB TOPPING (PAGE 17)

Preheat the oven to 400°F.

Heat the oil in a heavy-bottomed pot set over medium-high heat. Add the onions, garlic, and carrots and sauté until the mixture is dry, stirring frequently, 5 to 6 minutes. Add the vinegar and reduce slightly, 5 to 6 minutes. Add the tomatoes, basil, lemon zest, 1 tablespoon salt, ½ teaspoon pepper, and bread. Stir well to incorporate the bread, bring to a simmer, then lower the heat and cook, stirring frequently, until the juice has been absorbed by the bread, 25 to 30 minutes.

Transfer the mixture to a 2-quart baking dish. Sprinkle the bread crumb topping over the mixture. Bake in the oven until browned and bubbling, approximately 12 minutes.

Serve the tomatoes family style from the center of the table.

BLACK TRUFFLE
CREAMED SPINACH

SERVES 4

The combination of truffle oil and Parmigiano-Reggiano is so rich and steak-friendly that this dish is one of our customers' favorite sides—there's one on just about every table in our restaurants. It's a perfect example of how easy it is to make something traditional into something special. Everyone will recognize this as creamed spinach, but—I promise you—it'll be the best one they've ever tasted.

I POUND FRESH SPINACH, TRIMMED, WELL WASHED IN SEVERAL CHANGES OF COLD WATER AND LEFT A BIT DAMP, OR I POUND CHOPPED FROZEN SPINACH

2 CUPS HEAVY CREAM

1/2 POUND (2 STICKS) UNSALTED BUTTER, CUT INTO SMALL CUBES, SOFTENED AT ROOM TEMPERATURE

1/2 CUP GRATED PARMIGIANO-REGGIANO CHEESE (FROM ABOUT 2 OUNCES CHEESE)

1/4 CUP BLACK TRUFFLE OIL

2 TABLESPOONS BLACK TRUFFLE BUTTER, OPTIONAL

KOSHER SALT

FRESHLY GROUND BLACK PEPPER

Bring 1 1/2 cups water to a simmer in a large saucepan set over medium-high heat. Add the spinach, cover the pan, and steam for 3 to 4 minutes, lifting the lid periodically to stir up the spinach from the bottom. Remove the pan from the heat. When the spinach is cool enough to handle, squeeze out the excess water and finely chop it. (If using frozen spinach, there's no need to chop it further.)

Pour the cream into a large saucepan and bring to a simmer over medium heat. Let simmer, but not boil, until the cream is reduced by half, stirring frequently to make sure the cream doesn't scorch, approximately 10 minutes. Reduce the heat to low and stir in the butter slowly, a cube or two at a time, until well incorporated.

Add the spinach and stir until the spinach has absorbed the cream and butter. Add the Parmigiano-Reggiano, truffle oil, and truffle butter, if using. Season with 1 1/2 tablespoons salt and 2 teaspoons pepper and keep warm until serving. If the spinach looks dry, stir in water, a few drops at a time, until it reaches the desired consistency.

Here's a simpler variation of creamed spinach:

PARMESAN CREAMED SPINACH

I POUND FRESH SPINACH, TRIMMED,
WELL WASHED IN SEVERAL CHANGES
OF COLD WATER AND LEFT A BIT DAMP,
OR I POUND CHOPPED FROZEN SPINACH

I CUP HEAVY CREAM

2 TABLESPOONS UNSALTED BUTTER

½ CUP GRATED PARMIGIANO-
REGGIANO CHEESE (FROM ABOUT
2 OUNCES CHEESE)

FRESHLY GROUND BLACK PEPPER

KOSHER SALT

Bring 1½ cups water to a simmer in a large saucepan set over medium-high heat. Add the spinach, cover the pan, and steam for 3 to 4 minutes, lifting the lid periodically to stir the spinach up from the bottom. Remove the pan from the heat. When the leaves are cool enough to handle, squeeze out the excess water and finely chop it. (If using frozen spinach, there's no need to chop it further.)

Reduce the cream by half in a heavy-bottomed pot over medium heat. Add the spinach and stir to coat well with the cream. Cook while stirring over medium heat for 8 to 10 minutes. Add the butter and Parmigiano-Reggiano and stir over low heat until the creamed spinach is heated through. Add 2 teaspoons pepper and season to taste with salt.

COLLARD GREENS

SERVES 4 TO 6

One of the stalwarts of southern cooking—especially barbecue—is collard greens, an inexpensive, earthy-flavored, broad-leaved green whose durable texture lends itself to long cooking. Often cooked with garlic and bacon, collard greens are classic for a reason, so I don't mess around with them too much and instead cook them straight up with smoked bacon. The one touch I add is cider vinegar, one of the crucial ingredients in the barbecue sauce that collard greens are so often paired with.

2 TABLESPOONS CORN OIL OR OTHER NEUTRAL OIL SUCH AS GRAPESEED OR CANOLA

³/₄ CUP SLICED SMOKED BACON IN ¹/₄-INCH PIECES, OPTIONAL

I LARGE WHITE ONION, DICED

2 TABLESPOONS SLICED GARLIC

FRESHLY GROUND BLACK PEPPER

³/₄ CUP CIDER VINEGAR

2¹/₂ CUPS LOW-SODIUM, STORE-BOUGHT VEGETABLE OR CHICKEN BROTH

2 BUNCHES COLLARD GREENS, THICK STEMS REMOVED, CLEANED, AND ROUGHLY CHOPPED (ABOUT I2 CUPS CHOPPED)

KOSHER SALT

Heat the oil in a large, heavy-bottomed pot. If using, add the bacon and sauté until golden brown, 5 to 6 minutes. Add the onion and garlic and continue to cook for 3 minutes. Add 1 teaspoon pepper and toast it, stirring constantly. Next add the cider vinegar, broth, and greens. Season with 1 teaspoon salt and fold the greens into the liquid until the greens wilt. When the greens have wilted considerably, 7 to 8 minutes, reduce the heat to low, partially cover, and cook for 1¹/₂ hours. Taste and adjust the seasoning with more salt if necessary.

Serve from a bowl in the center of the table.

GLAZED BUTTERNUT SQUASH

WITH **MAPLE** AND **AUTUMN SPICES**

SERVES 8

A number of classic fall flavors come together in this side dish: squash, maple syrup, cinnamon, and star anise. What takes it to the steakhouse level is the addition of hot chile powder, which lends the squash a surprising heat that lets it get along with beef and other bold-flavored main courses.

I TEASPOON GROUND ALEPPO PEPPER OR ANCHO CHILE POWDER

2 TABLESPOONS GROUND CINNAMON

1/4 TEASPOON GROUND STAR ANISE

3/4 CUP MAPLE SYRUP

1/4 CUP LIGHT CORN SYRUP

1/4 CUP HONEY

I TABLESPOON MOLASSES

1/2 CUP LOW-SODIUM, STORE-BOUGHT VEGETABLE BROTH OR WATER

I TABLESPOON CHOPPED FRESH THYME LEAVES PLUS 8 SPRIGS THYME

FRESHLY GROUND BLACK PEPPER

KOSHER SALT

2 BUTTERNUT SQUASH, ABOUT 2 POUNDS EACH

8 FRESH FLAT-LEAF PARSLEY SPRIGS

I TEASPOON COARSE SEA SALT

Put the aleppo pepper, cinnamon, and star anise in a small bowl and stir them together.

Put the maple syrup, corn syrup, honey, molasses, broth, aleppo spice blend, chopped thyme, 1/4 teaspoon black pepper, and 1/2 teaspoon kosher salt in a small pot and bring to a simmer over medium heat. Continue to simmer until reduced by half, approximately 8 minutes. Remove the pot from the heat and set aside, covered, until needed.

Preheat the oven to 350°F.

Cut the butternut squash in half lengthwise and remove the seeds. Cut in half again where the "neck" and "belly" of the squash meet, so that you have 8 pieces total.

Using a small, sharp paring knife, score the flesh side of each piece of squash, making rows of cuts half an inch apart diagonally down the length of the squash. Then turn each piece and make half-inch cuts diagonally starting on the opposite side, so that each piece is scored with crosshatched cuts.

Set the squash pieces on a baking sheet, flesh side up. Using a pastry brush, generously coat the squash with the reduced glaze. Roast until tender to a knife tip, 55 to 60 minutes, basting every 15 minutes with additional glaze.

Serve warm from a platter or alongside poultry or meat, garnished with the parsley, thyme sprigs, and sea salt.

BATTER-FRIED ONIONS

SERVES 4

I think of these as onion rings 2.0. Two things take these a notch above your average onion rings. One is the shape, a bite-size, chip-like wedge. The other is the batter, seasoned with Spanish paprika, garlic powder, and cumin. The onion flavor is amped up by the addition of some of the onions' cooking liquid.

When you put the batter-coated onions in the oil, don't be too precise about it; ideally some fried onions will come out as chips, the rest as small, crunchy pieces.

2 LARGE WHITE ONIONS

I LARGE EGG

½ CUP MILK

½ CUP ALL-PURPOSE FLOUR

I TEASPOON BAKING POWDER

½ TEASPOON BAKING SODA

KOSHER SALT

2 TEASPOONS SWEET SPANISH PAPRIKA

¼ TEASPOON GARLIC POWDER

¼ TEASPOON GROUND CUMIN

6 CUPS CORN OIL OR OTHER NEUTRAL OIL SUCH AS GRAPESEED OR CANOLA

Peel the onions and trim off the ends. Cut each one in half lengthwise, then in half crosswise. Cut each quarter into quarters again, from stem to end. (When you cook them in the water, they will separate into "chips.")

Bring 2 quarts water to a boil in a large pot set over high heat. Add the onions and boil until soft and translucent, 10 to 12 minutes. Remove the pot from the heat and let the onions cool in the liquid. Scoop out ½ cup of the liquid and reserve. Let the onions soak in the remaining liquid.

In a small bowl mix the egg and milk thoroughly. Set aside.

Put the flour, baking powder, baking soda, 2 teaspoons salt, the paprika, garlic powder, and cumin in a medium bowl and stir together. Add the milk-egg mixture, whisking to incorporate. When thoroughly mixed, add a few tablespoons of the onion water to the batter to thin to the proper consistency—thin but with enough body to coat the onions. Drain the onions, add to the batter, and stir to coat well.

Heat the oil to 375°F in a 3-quart, deep-sided pot.

Remove the onions from the batter and allow the batter to lightly run off the onions. Fry small quantities (about 15 pieces per batch) for about 1½ minutes, then stir and fry for an additional 1½ minutes.

When a batch is fried and deep brown, remove from the oil with a mesh skimmer and set on absorbent paper towels. Taste one and season with salt if necessary.

If frying before the serving time, place the fried onions on a baking sheet in a 400°F oven to reheat for 3 to 4 minutes.

Transfer the onions to a plate, platter, or basket and serve hot.

GARLIC-PARMESAN POTATO CHIPS

SERVES 4 TO 6

My version of potato chips is rustic, which to me means pleasantly inconsistent: you know they're homemade by the slight variation in shape from chip to chip. Tossed with Parmesan cheese and garlic powder, these are powerfully flavored enough to be served with just about anything, especially grilled meats and burgers.

2 POUNDS IDAHO POTATOES (ABOUT 4 MEDIUM POTATOES)

6 CUPS CORN OIL OR OTHER NEUTRAL OIL SUCH AS GRAPESEED OR CANOLA

2½ TABLESPOONS FINELY GRATED PARMIGIANO-REGGIANO CHEESE (YOU CAN ALSO GRATE A WHOLE, 1-OUNCE PIECE OF CHEESE RIGHT ONTO THE CHIPS WHEN THEY COME OUT OF THE FRYER)

1 TEASPOON GARLIC POWDER

KOSHER SALT

Peel the potatoes and slice them crosswise into ⅛-inch-thick slices, preferably on a mandoline, gathering them in a bowl. Cover the slices with cold water.

BREAK POINT
The potatoes can be sliced and soaked for up to 24 hours. If soaking for more than 2 hours, cover and refrigerate them. When ready to cook, drain the potatoes and allow to air-dry on a kitchen towel for 25 minutes.

Heat the oil to 375°F in a 3-quart, deep-sided pot.

Add the potato slices in 2 or 3 batches and stir while frying until all are consistently browned, 7 to 8 minutes. As they are done, use a slotted spoon to transfer the chips to a paper-towel-lined plate.

When the oil has drained off onto the towel, transfer the hot chips to a large bowl. Scatter the Parmigiano-Reggiano over the hot chips, turning the chips to coat evenly. Season with the garlic powder and 1 teaspoon salt. Toss gently and serve hot.

GARLIC-HERB FRENCH FRIES

SERVES 4

My favorite way to enhance French fries used to be malt vinegar and sea salt, until I devised this little number. These fries are more intensely flavored than most, but the basic technique is the same as it is for all French fries, with two cooking stages: the potatoes are blanched and then fried. The garlic butter is made separately and tossed with the fries after they're cooked. If you own a squeeze bottle, use it to squirt the garlic butter over the fries; it's easy to coat as many of them as possible that way.

By the way, if you don't want to make your own fries, use the butter and garlic sauce to coat cooked frozen fries.

3 POUNDS IDAHO POTATOES (5 TO 6 LARGE POTATOES)

½ CUP CLARIFIED BUTTER (PAGE 16)

6 GARLIC CLOVES, THINLY SLICED

6 CUPS CORN OIL OR OTHER NEUTRAL OIL SUCH AS GRAPESEED OR CANOLA

2 TEASPOONS CHOPPED FRESH THYME LEAVES

KOSHER SALT

Peel the potatoes and trim off each rounded end so the potatoes can stand flat. Slice each one lengthwise into ¼-inch slices, then cut the slices lengthwise into ¼-inch fries.

Place in a bowl of cold water and soak for up to 1 day in advance of cooking. When ready to cook, drain the fries and air-dry them on a kitchen towel for 25 minutes.

Heat the clarified butter to 350°F in a small pot. Add the garlic and cook until golden brown, 3 to 4 minutes. Use a slotted spoon to remove the garlic chips from the butter and transfer them to an absorbent paper towel to crisp them. Reserve the garlic chips and the garlic butter separately.

Heat the oil to 325°F in a large, deep-sided pot. Blanch the French fries in small quantities for 4 minutes. As they are done, transfer them to a clean, absorbent towel or paper towels and let cool to room temperature.

Increase the heat of the oil to 375°F. Deep-fry the French fries in batches until dark golden brown while stirring, 7 to 8 minutes.

As they're done, gather the fries in a large bowl. If frying before the serving time, place the fries on a baking sheet in a 400°F oven to reheat for 3 to 4 minutes.

Season with 3 to 4 tablespoons of the butter and sprinkle with the garlic chips, thyme, and 1 teaspoon salt. Serve at once.

MASHED POTATOES
AND **LOBSTER, CHIVE, CHEDDAR,** AND **ROASTED GARLIC VARIATIONS**

SERVES 8 TO 10

There aren't many fish or meat dishes that aren't enhanced by mashed potatoes. Here's my recipe for this versatile side, along with four of my favorite variations. The lobster variation is practically a meal in itself. It makes a rich and luxurious side dish.

1¾ POUNDS IDAHO POTATOES (ABOUT 3 MEDIUM POTATOES)

KOSHER SALT

I CUP HEAVY CREAM, PLUS MORE IF NEEDED

4 TABLESPOONS (½ STICK) UNSALTED BUTTER

FRESHLY GROUND BLACK PEPPER

Put the potatoes in a pot. Add enough cold water to cover, then add 1 tablespoon salt. Bring the water to a boil, lower the heat, and cook the potatoes at a simmer until tender, approximately 35 minutes.

Drain the water from the pot, return the potatoes to the heat, and cook, stirring, to evaporate any lingering moisture. Transfer the potatoes to a mixing bowl.

Put the cream and butter in a small pot and bring to a simmer over medium heat. Pour half of the mixture over the potatoes and whip the potatoes with a hand mixer until smooth. When smooth, use a rubber spatula to fold the remaining cream-butter mixture into the potatoes until incorporated and smooth. Season with ¼ teaspoon pepper.

BREAK POINT
The mashed potatoes can be kept warm in a double-boiler set over simmering water for up to 2 hours. If the potatoes tighten up while resting, fold in additional hot cream before serving.

(CONTINUED)

Here are my favorite mashed potato variations:

CHEDDAR VARIATION

Whisk 4 ounces coarsely grated Cheddar cheese (about 1 cup grated) into the cream-butter mixture when it begins to simmer and finish making the potatoes. Transfer the potatoes to a 1-quart baking dish (about 9 inches by 5½ inches) and scatter 2 ounces grated Cheddar (about ½ cup grated) over the surface. Brown under the broiler, 3 to 4 minutes.

CHIVE VARIATION

Add ¾ cup minced fresh chives to the cream-butter mixture when it begins to simmer.

ROASTED GARLIC VARIATION

Stir 2 heads roasted, mashed garlic (see page 15) into the potatoes just before serving.

LOBSTER VARIATION

1¾ POUNDS IDAHO POTATOES (ABOUT 3 MEDIUM POTATOES)

KOSHER SALT

1 LOBSTER, 1¼ POUNDS

4 BAY LEAVES

1 LEMON, SLICED

1 TABLESPOON BLACK PEPPERCORNS

¼ CUP WHITE WINE VINEGAR

1 CUP HEAVY CREAM

4 TABLESPOONS (½ STICK) UNSALTED BUTTER

2 TABLESPOONS ROUGHLY CHOPPED FRESH TARRAGON LEAVES

FRESHLY GROUND BLACK PEPPER

Put the potatoes in a pot. Add enough cold water to cover, then add 1 tablespoon salt. Bring the water to a boil, lower the heat, and cook the potatoes at a simmer until tender, approximately 35 minutes.

Drain the water from the pot, return the potatoes to the heat, and cook, stirring, to evaporate any lingering moisture. Transfer the potatoes to a mixing bowl.

Kill the lobster by driving a sharp, heavy kitchen knife right between its eyes and pulling the knife forward and down, like a lever. This kills the lobster instantly and humanely.

Put 3 quarts water in a heavy-bottomed soup pot. Add the bay leaves, lemon slices, black peppercorns, and vinegar and bring to a boil over high heat. Fill a large bowl halfway with ice water. When the water boils, add the lobster and cook for 8 minutes. Use tongs to remove the lobster from the boiling water and submerge it in ice water to stop the cooking process quickly.

When cooled, separate the tail and claws from the body of the lobster. Use a mallet or the back of a heavy kitchen knife and crack the claws and "knuckles" of the lobster to remove the meat. Lay the tail on a flat surface and cut lengthwise. Catch all the juices, the tomalley, and any tiny bits of meat or shell in a heavy-bottomed saucepan. Dice the tail and claw meat into $\frac{1}{2}$-inch chunks and set aside.

Use a large, heavy knife to chop the carcass and shell of the lobster into small pieces, no bigger than an inch square.

Put the cream, $\frac{1}{4}$ cup water, and the butter in with the lobster juices and add the chopped lobster shell and the tarragon. Bring to a simmer and cook gently for 20 minutes, muddling with a wooden spoon to extract the maximum flavor from the shell. Strain through a fine sieve, pressing on the solids with the wooden spoon to extract all the liquid from the shells. Add half of the lobster cream to the cooked potatoes and whip with a mixer. Fold in the remaining cream and the diced lobster meat. Season to taste with salt and pepper. Cover and keep warm until ready to serve.

CRISP GOOSE FAT POTATOES

SERVES 4 TO 6

A small potato cake made crispy and crunchy by goose fat is the kind of decadent thing you expect at a steakhouse, and this over-the-top side dish is one of the you've-gotta-try-it specialties at Strip House. I don't often advocate going to the trouble of mail-ordering ingredients, but do what you must to get the goose or duck fat for this dish; it's worth the effort.

These are delicious with any grilled steaks, including Marinated Skirt Steak (page 120).

2 BAY LEAVES

8 FRESH THYME SPRIGS

4 FRESH ROSEMARY SPRIGS

KOSHER SALT

4 CUPS POTATOES IN MEDIUM DICE (FROM ABOUT 3 LARGE POTATOES, PEELED)

6 OUNCES (DRY WEIGHT) GOOSE OR DUCK FAT, ¾ CUP MELTED (SEE NOTE)

6 GARLIC CLOVES, CRACKED WITH THE SIDE OF A KNIFE, PLUS 5 GARLIC CLOVES, THINLY SLICED

FRESHLY GROUND BLACK PEPPER

UNSALTED BUTTER OR NONSTICK SPRAY FOR GREASING THE BAKING DISH

¼ CUP COARSELY CHOPPED FRESH FLAT-LEAF PARSLEY LEAVES

SEA SALT

Pour 8 cups water into a pot and bring to a boil over high heat. Sandwich the bay leaves between 4 of the thyme sprigs and 2 of the rosemary sprigs and gently but firmly tie them together with kitchen twine. Add the herbs and 1 tablespoon kosher salt to the pot. When the water boils, add the potatoes and boil until they are softened but still holding their shape, approximately 10 minutes. Drain the potatoes well, remove and discard the herbs, and set the potatoes aside.

Strip and chop the leaves from the remaining 4 thyme sprigs and 2 rosemary sprigs. Reserve the stems and set the chopped leaves aside. Put the goose fat, herb stems, cracked garlic, 1 teaspoon kosher salt, and ½ teaspoon pepper in a pot and bring to a simmer over medium-low heat. Reduce the heat to very low and cook very gently for 15 minutes, stirring occasionally to ensure that the garlic doesn't become too brown. (If the garlic is browning too quickly, turn off the heat and simply allow it to steep.) Remove the pan from the heat and let the garlic and herbs steep until needed.

Preheat the oven to 400°F. Strain and reserve the goose fat and discard the garlic and herbs.

Put the potatoes in a bowl. Add the chopped herb leaves and ⅓ cup of the goose fat and stir well. Some potatoes will break apart, some will hold their shape. Season the potato mixture with ¾ teaspoon kosher salt and ¼ teaspoon pepper.

Lightly grease a 1-pint baking dish with butter or nonstick spray. Pour the potato mixture into the dish, pressing it down firmly. Bake until the crust is light golden brown, 30 to 40 minutes. Let cool to room temperature, approximately 45 minutes, then cover with plastic wrap and refrigerate for 45 minutes to set.

BREAK POINT
The potato cake can be refrigerated overnight.

When ready to serve, preheat the oven to 375°F. Remove the potato cake from the mold and place on a baking sheet, bottom side up. Using a brush, baste the potato cake with the remaining goose fat. Bake until a deep golden brown, approximately 40 minutes, basting frequently.

To serve, lift the potato cake onto a serving platter and sprinkle the sliced garlic on the hot cake. Sprinkle with the sea salt and top with the chopped parsley. Serve immediately.

Note:
Goose and duck fat is available from specialty grocers and by mail order from D'Artagnan, www.dartagnan.com or 800–327–8246.

GRUYÈRE POTATO GRATIN

SERVES 8 TO 10

Of all the dishes in this book, few will fill your home with better aromas than this one: the roasted garlic and cooked Gruyère cheese will have everyone's appetite revved up by the time you serve it. The big flavor of this gratin comes from doubling up on the Gruyère; it's melted in the base and bands of it are layered between the potatoes.

Do not slice the potatoes ahead of time for this recipe. While it's usually okay to keep them in cold water, in this case it will rob them of the starch that is crucial to holding the gratin together.

3 CUPS HEAVY CREAM

10 ROASTED GARLIC CLOVES (PAGE 15), PUREED

12 OUNCES GRUYÈRE CHEESE, SLICED INTO ABOUT 18 SLICES, PLUS 8 OUNCES, GRATED (ABOUT 2½ CUPS GRATED)

KOSHER SALT

FRESHLY GROUND BLACK PEPPER

1 TEASPOON CHOPPED FRESH THYME LEAVES

3 POUNDS IDAHO POTATOES (ABOUT 6 LARGE POTATOES)

Pour the cream into a small pot and bring to a simmer over medium-high heat, but do not boil. Let simmer until reduced to 2½ cups, 6 to 8 minutes. Whisk in the garlic puree and grated Gruyère. Season with 1 teaspoon salt, 1 teaspoon pepper, and the thyme.

While the cream sauce is being prepared, peel the potatoes and slice them horizontally on a mandoline to a thickness of ⅛ inch. Add the cream mixture to the sliced potatoes in a bowl and mix well so that all the potato slices are coated.

Preheat the oven to 325°F.

In an 8 or 9 by 12-inch ovenproof casserole, layer about a third of the potato mixture and then a third of the sliced Gruyère cheese. Repeat the process two more times. Pour any remaining cream from the bowl onto the gratin. Lightly tap the casserole on the countertop to help the cream settle consistently throughout the gratin. Cover loosely with aluminum foil and bake for 1 hour. Remove the foil and bake for an additional 15 minutes to brown the top.

When cooked, the gratin should be golden brown on top and the potatoes should be tender to a knife tip.

Serve the gratin family style from the center of the table.

TOASTED BARLEY RISOTTO
WITH **MUSHROOMS** AND **THYME**

SERVES 6

Risotto is traditionally made with Arborio or other medium-grain Italian rice. This dish, in which barley is slow-cooked with gradual additions of broth, is based on the technique for making risotto. Barley has a lighter starch content, so the individual grains don't bind together as they do in a risotto, but the effect is very similar.

I CUP PEARL BARLEY (ABOUT 9 OUNCES)

¼ CUP CORN OIL OR OTHER NEUTRAL OIL SUCH AS GRAPESEED OR CANOLA

½ CUP FINELY DICED WHITE ONIONS

¾ CUP THINLY SLICED CREMINI MUSHROOMS (FROM 8 OR 9 MUSHROOMS)

I MEDIUM PORTOBELLO MUSHROOM, GILLS REMOVED WITH A PARING KNIFE OR TABLESPOON, FINELY DICED

I SMALL BUNCH OYSTER MUSHROOMS, CHOPPED (ABOUT 1½ CUPS CHOPPED)

2 TABLESPOONS THINLY SLICED GARLIC

¼ CUP WHITE WINE (OAKY AND RICH, LIKE A CHARDONNAY)

I TEASPOON CHOPPED FRESH THYME LEAVES

KOSHER SALT

FRESHLY GROUND BLACK PEPPER

5 CUPS LOW-SODIUM, STORE-BOUGHT CHICKEN BROTH OR WATER, PLUS MORE IF NEEDED

¼ CUP HEAVY CREAM

½ CUP FINELY GRATED PARMIGIANO-REGGIANO CHEESE (FROM ABOUT 2 OUNCES CHEESE)

In a dry sauté pan, toast the barley on the stove over high heat, stirring constantly, until lightly browned, 6 to 7 minutes.

In a pot, heat the oil and sauté the onions, mushrooms, and garlic until soft, 8 to 9 minutes. Add the toasted barley to the pot, then add the white wine, thyme, 1 tablespoon salt, 1 teaspoon pepper, and broth. Bring to a boil, then reduce the heat and simmer gently for 45 minutes over medium-high heat. If the liquid boils away, stir in more broth, ¼ cup at a time.

When the barley is soft and tender, stir in the cream and cook for 2 to 3 minutes while stirring. Stir in the Parmigiano-Reggiano cheese and serve.

MICHAEL'S
MACARONI AND CHEESE

SERVES 6 TO 8

One of the most popular buzzwords on menus these days is "comfort food," and there's nothing more comforting than macaroni and cheese. Here, it's turned into a sophisticated dish made with a béchamel (a white sauce of milk and flour) that's amped up with Cheddar, Gorgonzola, and Parmigiano-Reggiano. But it's recognizable as macaroni and cheese because I use the classic macaroni pasta and top it with bread crumbs after the traditional style. We serve this at Michael Jordan's The Steak House NYC, where it's a favorite.

This is a perfect accompaniment to grilled dishes, such as any of the steak recipes in the book or Lemon-Pepper Marinated Chicken (page 108). It's also delicious on its own.

KOSHER SALT

1/2 POUND ELBOW MACARONI

1 TABLESPOON VEGETABLE OIL

1/2 CUP FINELY DICED ONIONS

2 TABLESPOONS UNSALTED BUTTER, PLUS MORE FOR GREASING THE BAKING DISH

1/4 CUP ALL-PURPOSE FLOUR

3 CUPS MILK

1 TABLESPOON WORCESTERSHIRE SAUCE

2 TABLESPOONS DIJON MUSTARD

FRESHLY GROUND BLACK PEPPER

2 1/2 CUPS GRATED AGED WHITE CHEDDAR CHEESE (FROM ABOUT 10 OUNCES CHEESE)

1/2 CUP CRUMBLED GORGONZOLA CHEESE (FROM ABOUT 2 1/2 OUNCES CHEESE)

3/4 CUP FINELY GRATED PARMIGIANO-REGGIANO CHEESE (FROM ABOUT 12 OUNCES CHEESE)

1/4 CUP SOUR CREAM

1/2 CUP FRESH BREAD CRUMBS

If serving immediately, preheat the oven to 400°F.

Bring a large pot of salted water to a boil over high heat. Add the macaroni and cook until al dente, 6 to 7 minutes. Drain the macaroni in a fine-mesh strainer and cool under cold, running water. Drain again and set aside.

Meanwhile, heat the vegetable oil in a nonstick sauté pan over medium-low heat. Add the onions and sauté until softened but not browned, approximately 4 minutes. Remove the pan from the heat and set aside.

Melt the butter in a large, heavy-bottomed pot over medium heat. Add the flour and stir to incorporate it thoroughly, working out any lumps. Cook, stirring constantly, for 3 to 4 minutes, until the mixture is well blended and starts to dry slightly; do not allow it to darken.

Slowly whisk the milk into the mixture and continue to whisk until the béchamel is smooth and begins to thicken, 7 to 8 minutes. Stir in the onions, Worcestershire sauce, mustard, 1/2 teaspoon salt, and 1/4 teaspoon pepper. Continue to whisk until all the ingredients are incorporated.

Begin to add the Cheddar cheese gradually in small amounts, whisking to help melt the cheese. Add the Gorgonzola and ½ cup of the Parmigiano-Reggiano, again whisking until smooth.

BREAK POINT

You can keep the béchamel and pasta separate, covered, and warm or at room temperature for up to 2 hours. Preheat the oven to 400°F if you haven't already.

Mix the cooked macaroni and sour cream into the cheese béchamel. Transfer the mixture to a buttered 8 by 12-inch (or 3-quart) baking dish. Top with the bread crumbs and then the remaining ¼ cup Parmigiano-Reggiano.

Bake for 10 to 15 minutes, until hot and the top is browned. If the top isn't browned enough, finish under the broiler for a few minutes.

Serve the macaroni from the baking dish in the center of the table.

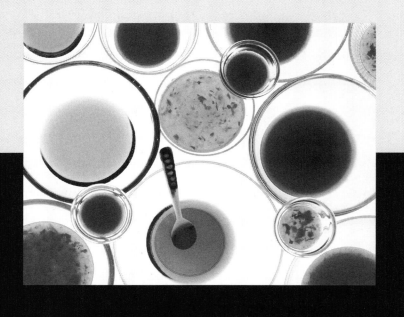

CONDIMENTS AND SAVORY SAUCES

Quick and Easy Ways to Take Things to a Whole New Level

Creative, flavorful sauces are a surefire way to jazz up any meal. Whether you make them yourself or keep bottles of prepared sauces in the refrigerator, it's always a good idea to have a variety on tap. For that reason, most of the recipes in this chapter produce relatively small quantities, the idea being that none of them takes up too much space in the fridge, so you can make and store several.

I've put these recipes in a chapter all their own because as far as I'm concerned a great sauce or condiment is just as valuable as any other recipe. Maybe more so: if you know how to poach a piece of fish, roast a chicken, or grill a steak, a sauce is all you need to make those and other staples into something different every time you serve them.

This chapter features all of my favorite sauces, from must-have classics like hollandaise and béarnaise to my own inventions, like Jalapeño–Tropical Fruit Steak Sauce, Smoked Chile Ketchup, and Mango-Cumin Cream.

A lot of my sauces are based on the valuable lesson I learned from Mark Miller, the southwestern master chef for whom I worked early in my career. Mark taught me about the sauces of Mexico, which have a depth and purity of flavor as well as a complexity and balance that surpass most of the ones we produce north of the border.

As with the side dishes in the previous chapter, I suggest you do as we do in my steakhouses, and my home, and serve a number of sauces alongside any main course, letting everyone pick and choose his or her own pairings, perhaps sampling several in one sitting.

COCKTAIL SAUCE

MAKES 2 CUPS

Once you make your own cocktail sauce, you may never use store-bought again.

2 TEASPOONS CORN OIL OR OTHER NEUTRAL OIL SUCH AS GRAPESEED OR CANOLA

I GARLIC CLOVE, ROUGHLY CHOPPED

I POUND FRESH PLUM TOMATOES, CORED AND ROUGHLY CHOPPED

3 TABLESPOONS TOMATO PASTE

I CUP PACKED LIGHT BROWN SUGAR

1/4 CUP CORN SYRUP

1/2 CUP WHITE WINE VINEGAR

1 1/2 TABLESPOONS WORCESTERSHIRE SAUCE

2 TABLESPOONS TABASCO SAUCE

1/4 TEASPOON GROUND CLOVES

1/4 CUP PREPARED HORSERADISH

ABOUT I TABLESPOON FRESHLY SQUEEZED LEMON JUICE

Heat a medium saucepan over high heat. Pour in the corn oil and let it heat up for 1 minute. Add the garlic and sauté until golden brown, 1 to 2 minutes. Add the tomatoes, tomato paste, brown sugar, corn syrup, vinegar, Worcestershire, Tabasco, and cloves and bring the sauce to a boil. Reduce to a simmer and let simmer until reduced by one-third, 5 to 7 minutes.

Remove the pot from the heat and let cool for 5 to 10 minutes. Pour the mixture into a blender and blend until smooth. Stir in the horseradish, season with the lemon juice, cover, and chill overnight before serving. The sauce can be covered and refrigerated for up to 3 days. Whisk the sauce well just before serving.

RED CHILE COCKTAIL SAUCE

MAKES 1¾ CUPS

Use the salt, not the amount of chile, to adjust the heat of this sauce. The salt enhances the heat of the peppers, so season carefully until it pleases your palate.

3 TABLESPOONS ANCHO CHILE PUREE (FROM 1 DRIED ANCHO CHILE; SEE NOTE)

½ CANNED CHIPOTLE IN ADOBO PLUS 1 TABLESPOON ADOBO SAUCE

1½ CUPS KETCHUP

2 TABLESPOONS PREPARED HORSERADISH

3 TABLESPOONS FRESHLY SQUEEZED LIME JUICE

1 TEASPOON GROUND CUMIN

3 TABLESPOONS FINELY DICED SHALLOTS

3 TABLESPOONS WORCESTERSHIRE SAUCE

KOSHER SALT

Blend the ancho and chipotle to a paste in a blender. Transfer to a small bowl, scraping down the sides of the blender with a spatula. Add the remaining ingredients and salt to taste, stir, cover, and refrigerate for at least 2 hours before serving.

Note: To Make Dried Chile Puree

Preheat the oven to 400°F. Roast the whole dried chile on the center rack for 3 to 4 minutes, until it browns and becomes fragrant and puffy. Remove the chile from the oven. Once it's cool enough to handle, 5 to 6 minutes, remove the stem and shake out and discard the seeds. Put the seedless, roasted chile in a small saucepan of cold water and bring to a boil over medium-high heat. Let boil for 3 to 4 minutes, then use tongs to remove the chile from the water. Reserve the water, unless it has become bitter, in which case you should discard it and use fresh water for the puree.

Tear the chile into small pieces and put them in a blender along with ½ to ¾ cup of the reserved boiling water. Puree on high speed until smooth, 1 to 2 minutes.

MINCED VEGETABLE
TARTAR SAUCE

MAKES 2 CUPS

This tartar sauce takes its cue from vegetable cream cheese, adding carrot, celery, and onion to the classic tartar formula.

I CUP SOUR CREAM

½ CUP MAYONNAISE

2 TABLESPOONS MINCED CORNICHONS PLUS 2 TABLESPOONS CORNICHON JUICE

2 TABLESPOONS MINCED RED ONION

I TABLESPOON MINCED FRESH DILL FRONDS

3 TABLESPOONS MINCED CARROT

3 TABLESPOONS SCRAPED, MINCED CELERY

ZEST OF I LEMON

½ TEASPOON KOSHER SALT

¼ TEASPOON FRESHLY GROUND BLACK PEPPER

Stir all the ingredients together in a bowl, cover, and refrigerate for 1 to 2 hours before serving.

RÉMOULADE

MAKES ¾ CUP

Rémoulade is a variant of the better-known tartar sauce; it's similar, but where tartar tastes of dill, the herbs aren't as forward here. Rémoulade is more complex in flavor, with additional ingredients like capers, mustard, and paprika.

½ CUP MAYONNAISE

I TABLESPOON FINELY CHOPPED CAPERS PLUS I TEASPOON CAPER JUICE (IF USING SALT-PACKED CAPERS, RINSE THEM FIRST)

I½ TEASPOONS DIJON MUSTARD

I TEASPOON SWEET SPANISH PAPRIKA

I TEASPOON GRATED LEMON ZEST

½ TEASPOON TABASCO SAUCE

I TABLESPOON CHOPPED FRESH CHERVIL LEAVES, OPTIONAL

I TABLESPOON THINLY SLICED FRESH CHIVES

Stir all the ingredients together in a bowl, cover, and refrigerate for 1 to 2 hours before serving.

MIGNONETTE

MAKES ½ CUP

This is the classic version of the sauce traditionally spooned over a variety of oysters or raw shellfish. The pepper, red wine vinegar, and shallots seem to bring out the best in any variety.

3 TABLESPOONS VERY FINELY DICED SHALLOTS

I TEASPOON CRACKED BLACK PEPPERCORNS

¼ CUP RED WINE VINEGAR

2 TABLESPOONS WATER

½ TEASPOON SUGAR

½ TEASPOON KOSHER SALT

Stir all the ingredients together in a bowl, cover, and refrigerate for 1 to 2 hours before serving.

CUCUMBER VARIATION

This is delicious on sweet Olympia or Kumamoto oysters, as well as very delicate lump crabmeat or lobster meat. The freshness of the cucumber puree works well with the fresh, oceanic flavor of chilled seafood.

Peel and seed 1 large cucumber and chop part of it into ½ cup very tiny dice. Set aside the small dice and roughly chop the remaining cucumber. Add the roughly chopped cucumber pieces to a blender with ¼ cup cold water and puree until smooth. Add this to the mignonette made with ½ teaspoon cracked black peppercorns and ½ teaspoon kosher salt. Chill before serving.

CHIPOTLE CHILE MAYONNAISE

MAKES I GENEROUS CUP

This sauce has a distinct southwestern flavor thanks to the chipotle chile. The smoky flavor and the lime's acidity make it a perfect ally for grilled pork, chicken, and lobster, adding zest to chicken salad, and as a condiment for all kinds of sandwiches.

I CUP MAYONNAISE

2 TEASPOONS FINELY GRATED LIME ZEST PLUS 2 TEASPOONS FRESHLY SQUEEZED LIME JUICE

3 TABLESPOONS PUREED CANNED CHIPOTLES IN ADOBO (FROM ABOUT 2 PEPPERS)

Mix all the ingredients together thoroughly in a small bowl. Refrigerate for 1 hour before serving.

This mayonnaise can be covered and refrigerated for up to 3 days.

MANGO-CUMIN CREAM

MAKES ABOUT 3 CUPS

Sweet and hot, with a pronounced cumin tinge and the fragrant blast of cilantro, this sauce has many applications, such as a dressing for poached shrimp and lobster. Use it sparingly; a little goes a long way.

3 JALAPEÑOS

I MANGO

$\frac{1}{4}$ CUP FRESHLY SQUEEZED LIME JUICE

$1\frac{1}{2}$ CUPS SOUR CREAM

$\frac{1}{2}$ TEASPOON KOSHER SALT

$\frac{1}{2}$ TEASPOON CRACKED BLACK PEPPER

2 TABLESPOONS THINLY SLICED FRESH MINT LEAVES

I TABLESPOON GROUND CUMIN

2 TABLESPOONS THINLY SLICED FRESH CILANTRO LEAVES

Roast the jalapeños by placing them over the flame of a gas stove and turning frequently with tongs until charred. When cool enough to handle, peel off and discard the charred skin and seed the jalapeños. Dice the flesh and then pulverize it with the blade of the knife against the cutting board. Set aside. (If you don't have a gas stove, broil the jalapeños for 4 to 5 minutes, turning over once, until the skin is blackened and begins to pull away.)

Peel the mango and slice the flesh off the large central pit. Cut part of it into $\frac{1}{2}$ cup very fine dice. Roughly chop the remaining mango (about 1 cup chopped) and put it in a blender with the lime juice and $\frac{1}{2}$ cup water. Blend until smoothly pureed.

Put the mango puree in a medium bowl and blend in the jalapeños and remaining ingredients. Chill before serving.

HORSERADISH CREAM

MAKES 2½ CUPS

This is a classic horseradish cream, in which the flavors are punched up by a generous dose of lemon zest. Use it on smoked salmon, red meat, and chicken (it's especially good with chicken paillard), or drizzle it over lentil soup. It is also a great dip for vegetables.

2 CUPS SOUR CREAM

½ CUP PREPARED HORSERADISH

I TABLESPOON GRATED LEMON ZEST

I TEASPOON KOSHER SALT

I TEASPOON MINCED FRESH THYME LEAVES

½ TEASPOON FRESHLY GROUND BLACK PEPPER

Stir all the ingredients together well in a bowl. Cover and refrigerate for 1 to 2 hours to chill the sauce and give the flavors a chance to mingle.

The sauce can be covered and refrigerated for up to 3 days.

GRILLED
SUMMER FRUIT RELISH

MAKES 1½ CUPS

This spicy, chunky condiment for chicken and fatty fish like salmon is loaded with rich, bright, clean, spicy flavors. Like many of my favorite recipes, it packs a lot of sensory action into one place. I'm big on alternatives and using whatever's available, especially during the summer, when you're likely to have different fruits on your counter or in your refrigerator on different days. You can make this with nectarines, pineapple, or fresh apricots in place of the plums and peach.

½ JALAPEÑO

4 RIPE PLUMS, PITTED AND SLICED INTO WEDGES

I RIPE PEACH, PITTED AND SLICED INTO WEDGES

4 FRESH MINT LEAVES, VERY THINLY SLICED

2 TEASPOONS FINELY CHOPPED FRESH CILANTRO LEAVES

ZEST AND JUICE OF I LIME

2 TEASPOONS SUGAR

Roast the jalapeño by placing it over the flame of a gas stove, turning frequently with tongs until charred. When cool enough to handle, peel off and discard the charred skin and seed the pepper. Dice the flesh. Set aside.

Prepare a well-cleaned, seasoned grill for grilling or preheat a cast-iron pan on a stovetop over high heat. (See pages 96–100. Do not use a grill pan.) Add the plum and peach wedges, in batches if necessary, and grill until softened and the sugars have caramelized to brown the flesh, 5 to 6 minutes, depending on the ripeness of the fruit and the heat of the grill. (It should take 2 to 3 minutes in a cast-iron pan; you won't have grill marks but will see marked caramelization.) Do not overcook; you don't want the fruit to be mushy.

Dice the grilled fruits and put in a small bowl. Add the jalapeño and remaining ingredients and refrigerate for at least 30 minutes or up to 4 hours before serving, but no longer—you want the flavors to stay vibrant.

JALAPEÑO–TROPICAL FRUIT
STEAK SAUCE

MAKES 3½ CUPS

This sweet and hot sauce is addictively head-blowing, thanks to the fact that the jalapeño seeds and membranes are left intact. Pay close attention to the timing with this one: the mango mixture should cool just slightly before the jalapeño puree is stirred in, and it should be cooked no longer than 1 minute after the slurry is added, to keep the jalapeño and cilantro tasting fresh and uncooked.

Jalapeños and other chiles vary greatly in intensity, so taste or add them gradually, especially in recipes like this one that call for relatively large quantities.

6 JALAPEÑOS, STEMMED AND ROUGHLY CHOPPED

¼ CUP FRESH CILANTRO LEAVES

I CUP MANGO PUREE (FROM ½ TO ¾ FRESH MANGO, PIT REMOVED)

I CUP PASSION FRUIT PUREE (FROM ABOUT 6 PASSION FRUITS, HALVED AND PRESSED THROUGH A SIEVE WITH THE BACK OF A WOODEN SPOON)

¾ CUP ORANGE JUICE

¾ CUP GRAPEFRUIT JUICE

¼ CUP PACKED LIGHT BROWN SUGAR

½ CUP DISTILLED WHITE VINEGAR

2 TABLESPOONS CORNSTARCH

Put the jalapeños, cilantro, and ¾ cup water in a blender and puree until smooth. Set aside.

Put the mango puree, passion fruit puree, orange juice, grape-fruit juice, brown sugar, and vinegar in a heavy-bottomed saucepan. Bring to a simmer over medium heat and reduce to 2 cups, approximately 40 minutes. Remove the pan from the heat and allow to cool slightly, then fold in the jalapeño mixture.

Stir the cornstarch and 2 tablespoons water together in a small bowl, then stir into the mango–passion fruit reduction. Return to the heat and cook, stirring, for 1 minute. Remove from the heat and chill quickly by placing the bowl in the freezer for about 5 minutes, but no longer.

STEAKHOUSE SAUCE

MAKES 1 QUART

This dark blend of sweet and spicy flavors pairs well with a salty char and makes a big impact even with the most powerfully flavored meats.

The recipe makes a quart of sauce. When you assemble this many ingredients, you want to have more than a cup to show for the trouble. This will keep for up to one week in the refrigerator.

1 TABLESPOON CORN OIL OR OTHER NEUTRAL OIL SUCH AS GRAPESEED OR CANOLA

1 CUP FINELY DICED WHITE ONIONS

2 TABLESPOONS MINCED GARLIC

2 CUPS CANNED WHOLE PLUM TOMATOES, WITH THEIR JUICE, ROUGHLY CHOPPED

1/2 CUP MOLASSES

1/2 CUP PREPARED HORSERADISH

1/4 CUP TOMATO PASTE

1 1/2 TEASPOONS GRATED ORANGE ZEST

1 1/2 TEASPOONS MINCED FRESH THYME LEAVES

1/2 CUP WORCESTERSHIRE SAUCE

1/4 CUP PACKED LIGHT BROWN SUGAR

3/4 CUP RED WINE VINEGAR

2 TEASPOONS CAYENNE PEPPER

Heat the oil in a heavy-bottomed pot over medium-high heat. Add the onions and garlic and cook until softened but not browned, approximately 4 minutes. Add the tomatoes and their juice, then add the remaining ingredients and cook over medium heat, stirring occasionally, until slightly thickened, 20 to 25 minutes.

Remove the pot from the heat and let cool. Transfer to an airtight container and chill before using. This sauce will keep in the refrigerator for up to 1 week.

SMOKED CHILE KETCHUP

MAKES ABOUT 2 CUPS

The rich, bold flavor of chipotle chiles stands up very well to grilled foods, from shellfish to steaks. Thanks to the corn syrup and brown sugar, there's a nice, sweet balance here.

2 TABLESPOONS CORN OIL OR OTHER NEUTRAL OIL SUCH AS GRAPESEED OR CANOLA

²/₃ CUP ROUGHLY CHOPPED WHITE ONIONS

2 GARLIC CLOVES, THINLY SLICED

½ CUP ROASTED TOMATOES (PAGE 16), CHOPPED

1 TABLESPOON MINCED FRESH THYME LEAVES

¾ CUP LIGHT CORN SYRUP

¼ CUP SHERRY VINEGAR

¼ CUP PACKED LIGHT BROWN SUGAR

¼ CUP CHIPOTLE CHILE PUREE (FROM ABOUT 6 DRIED CHIPOTLES; SEE NOTE ON PAGE 174)

1 TABLESPOON KOSHER SALT

Pour the corn oil into a large, heavy-bottomed saucepan and set over medium heat. Add the onions and garlic and cook until softened but not browned, approximately 4 minutes. Add the tomatoes and all the remaining ingredients and simmer, stirring occasionally, until the tomatoes break down and the sauce is slightly thickened, approximately 20 minutes. Transfer the mixture to a blender and puree.

The ketchup can be covered and refrigerated for up to 3 days.

RED ONION COMPOTE

MAKES 1½ CUPS

A sweet, fragrant, and tangy compote made by stewing down onions with herbs, spices, and vinegar, this is delicious alongside everything from poultry to steaks and is especially good with scallops, grilled fish, and filet mignon.

2 TABLESPOONS CORN OIL OR OTHER NEUTRAL OIL SUCH AS GRAPESEED OR CANOLA

1 TABLESPOON GROUND CORIANDER

3 CUPS FINELY DICED RED ONIONS (FROM ABOUT 3 MEDIUM ONIONS)

1 TABLESPOON GRATED ORANGE ZEST

2 BAY LEAVES

¾ TEASPOON GROUND JUNIPER BERRIES

1 CUP SUGAR

2 CUPS RED WINE

½ CUP RED WINE VINEGAR

1 TEASPOON CHOPPED FRESH THYME LEAVES

1 CUP ORANGE JUICE

Heat the oil in a heavy-bottomed saucepan over medium heat. Add the coriander and sauté until fragrant, approximately 30 seconds. Add all the remaining ingredients. Bring to a boil, then reduce to a simmer. Cook for 1 hour, stirring occasionally, until the mixture attains the consistency of a thick relish or chutney. Stir frequently for the last 20 minutes of cooking time.

The sauce can be cooled, covered, and refrigerated for up to 3 days. Before serving, let it come to room temperature or gently warm it in a water bath.

STILTON CHEESE SAUCE

MAKES 1¾ CUPS

This intense cheese sauce for red meats, poultry, and open-faced burgers uses the powerful blue cheese Stilton and combines it with white wine, garlic, and herbs. It's essentially a fondue that's been slightly thinned with water and cream so that it can be poured. Feel free to use other blue cheeses in place of the Stilton.

2 TABLESPOONS CORN OIL OR OTHER NEUTRAL OIL SUCH AS GRAPESEED OR CANOLA

¼ CUP FINELY DICED WHITE ONION

1 TABLESPOON MINCED GARLIC

½ CUP DRY WHITE WINE

1 CUP HEAVY CREAM

10 OUNCES STILTON CHEESE, CRUMBLED (ABOUT 2 CUPS)

½ TEASPOON MINCED FRESH THYME LEAVES

¼ TEASPOON GRATED LEMON ZEST

KOSHER SALT

FRESHLY GROUND BLACK PEPPER

Heat the oil in a heavy-bottomed pot set over medium-high heat. Add the onion and garlic and cook until softened but not browned, approximately 4 minutes. Pour in the wine, raise the heat to high, and cook until reduced by half, 3 to 4 minutes. Add the cream and ¼ cup water and cook until reduced by one-third, approximately 6 minutes. Stir in half the cheese. Whisk until incorporated and the sauce is somewhat smooth. Add the thyme and zest.

Remove the pot from the heat and let cool slightly, then fold in the remaining cheese. Season with ¼ teaspoon salt and ¼ teaspoon pepper.

The sauce can be covered and refrigerated for up to 6 hours. The crumbled cheese will melt when reheated, so add some more cheese to preserve its texture.

Serve warm.

HOLLANDAISE

MAKES 1¼ CUPS

Along with bordelaise, hollandaise is probably the best-known steak sauce, a rich blend of egg yolks, clarified butter, and flavorings like Worcestershire and lemon juice. Not only is it delicious in its own right, but variations like béarnaise and Choron are useful to have in your repertoire.

2 LARGE EGG YOLKS

1½ CUPS WARM CLARIFIED BUTTER (PAGE 16)

¼ TEASPOON WORCESTERSHIRE SAUCE

½ TEASPOON TABASCO SAUCE

1 TEASPOON FRESHLY SQUEEZED LEMON JUICE

KOSHER SALT

FRESHLY GROUND WHITE PEPPER

Put the egg yolks in a medium stainless-steel bowl. Set over a hot water bath and whisk the eggs to a froth. Add 1 tablespoon hot water from the bath and whisk the yolks for 30 seconds to further heat the eggs. Gradually whisk in the clarified butter, then another tablespoon of hot water. Whisk in the Worcestershire sauce, Tabasco, lemon juice, 1 teaspoon salt, and ½ teaspoon pepper.

BONUS POINTS

BÉARNAISE SAUCE

5 SHALLOTS, VERY FINELY DICED (ABOUT 1 CUP DICED)

¼ CUP MINCED FRESH TARRAGON LEAVES (FROM ABOUT 12 SPRIGS)

1½ TEASPOONS CRACKED BLACK PEPPER

1 CUP RED WINE

1 CUP RED WINE VINEGAR

Put all the ingredients in a pot, bring to a boil, lower to a simmer, and reduce to ½ cup, approximately 20 minutes. Let cool, then whisk into the egg yolks and proceed with the hollandaise sauce.

SAUCE CHORON

Sauce Choron is hollandaise sauce with chopped roasted tomatoes stirred in. Add ⅓ cup chopped Roasted Tomatoes (page 16) and 1 tablespoon béarnaise reduction to the egg yolks and proceed with the hollandaise recipe.

TARRAGON-MUSTARD SAUCE

MAKES 1¾ CUPS

Tarragon is the herb most closely associated with lobster, so serve this sauce warm with seafood, steamed lobster, firm-fleshed white fish like halibut, or poultry.

2 TABLESPOONS CORN OIL OR OTHER NEUTRAL OIL SUCH AS GRAPESEED OR CANOLA

3 SHALLOTS, THINLY SLICED

3 GARLIC CLOVES, THINLY SLICED

½ CUP FRESH TARRAGON LEAVES

¾ CUP DRY WHITE WINE

½ CUP DIJON MUSTARD

1¾ CUPS BEEF STOCK (PAGE 14)

1 CUP LOW-SODIUM, STORE-BOUGHT CHICKEN BROTH

2 TABLESPOONS UNSALTED BUTTER

FRESHLY GROUND BLACK PEPPER

KOSHER SALT

Pour the oil into a heavy-bottomed saucepan and heat over medium heat. Add the shallots and garlic and cook until browned, approximately 5 minutes.

Add the tarragon and wine. Raise the heat to high, bring to a boil, and reduce the wine by half, approximately 5 minutes. Transfer the mixture to a blender and puree until smooth, with no visible bits of tarragon left, then return to the hot pot.

Stir in the mustard, beef stock, and chicken broth. Bring to a boil over high heat, then lower the heat and simmer until the mixture coats the back of a wooden spoon, 30 minutes.

BREAK POINT
The sauce can be made to this point, cooled, covered, and refrigerated for up to 3 days. Re-warm over low heat.

Stir in the butter and ½ teaspoon pepper and season to taste with salt.

BORDELAISE SAUCE

MAKES 1½ CUPS

This is one of the all-time most popular sauces in Western cooking. Try to find a high-quality demi-glace or veal stock (available from gourmet markets and specialty stores); it makes a big difference in whether the sauce has the proper body. If ever there was a time to make your own beef stock.

2 CUPS SHALLOTS, UNPEELED, ROUGHLY CHOPPED

2 HEADS GARLIC, UNPEELED, ROUGHLY CHOPPED

12 FRESH THYME SPRIGS

2 CUPS ROUGHLY CHOPPED BUTTON MUSHROOMS (FROM ABOUT 5 OUNCES MUSHROOMS)

4 BAY LEAVES

2½ CUPS RED WINE

¼ CUP PLUS 1 TABLESPOON DEMI-GLACE OR 1 QUART RICH VEAL STOCK OR HOMEMADE BEEF STOCK (PAGE 14)

1 QUART LOW-SODIUM, STORE-BOUGHT CHICKEN BROTH

3 TABLESPOONS UNSALTED BUTTER, CUT INTO 3 PIECES

Combine the shallots, garlic, thyme, mushrooms, bay leaves, and red wine in a bowl, cover, and refrigerate for 2 to 3 hours.

Preheat the oven to 400°F.

Spread the mixture out in a roasting pan and roast, stirring occasionally, until the wine has reduced by about half and the mixture thickens considerably, 40 to 45 minutes.

Remove the pan from the oven and transfer the mixture to a saucepan. Add the demi-glace and chicken broth. Bring to a boil over high heat, then lower the heat and simmer until thickened, 50 to 60 minutes.

Strain the sauce through a fine-mesh strainer set over a bowl, pressing down on the solids to extract as much liquid as possible. Measure the sauce. If you have more than 1½ cups, return the liquid to the stove over high heat and continue to reduce until the sauce is thickened to a near-syrup consistency and "tacky."

BREAK POINT
The sauce can be made to this point, cooled, covered, and refrigerated for up to 3 days, or frozen for up to 3 weeks. Defrost and gently reheat before proceeding.

Just before serving, whisk in the butter, 1 piece at a time.

DESSERTS

One More Thing

If you want to see something funny, eavesdrop on a table of steakhouse customers when their waiter shows up with the dessert menus. That moment is the ultimate match between the brain, which knows the appetite has been more than sated, and the taste buds, which crave something sweet to punctuate the meal and bring it to a fitting close.

If you want to win a bet, put your money on the taste buds; they *always* win. Everyone has dessert in a steakhouse, even if it means one dessert and four spoons, a very common request.

As with the starters and sides that precede and accompany the main courses in this book, the desserts in this chapter are fashioned after classic dishes, but with a bit of a twist. Here you'll find my versions of cheesecake, chocolate cake, key lime pie, strawberry shortcake, and so on, exactly the kind of things you want after a steakhouse-style feast.

There are also a handful of recipes for toppings and sauces intended to complement store-bought ice creams. As with this book's make-your-own martinis and many of the table-share appetizers, my preferred way to serve them is to set them out and let everyone make his or her own sundae, the ultimate mix-and-match indulgence.

STRAWBERRY "BISCUITCAKE"

SERVES 8 TO 10

One of the classic all-American desserts, strawberry shortcake is a marvel of simplicity, with strawberries, pastry, and whipped cream in perfect balance. I stay very true to tradition on the flavor front, making this version visually surprising: a cluster of biscuits is arranged in a cake pan and baked into an interlocking pattern. The entire cake is then sliced in half, filled with berries and cream, and reassembled. For maximum effect, present the whole cake at the table and cut it into individual servings there.

2 PINTS RIPE STRAWBERRIES, STEMMED AND QUARTERED

$\frac{1}{4}$ CUP PLUS 1 TABLESPOON GRANULATED SUGAR

3 TABLESPOONS COLD UNSALTED BUTTER, CUT INTO SMALL PIECES, PLUS MORE FOR GREASING THE PAN

3 CUPS ALL-PURPOSE FLOUR

1 TABLESPOON BAKING POWDER

1 TEASPOON FINE SALT

1 CUP HEAVY CREAM PLUS 2 CUPS WHIPPED UNTIL FIRM

$\frac{3}{4}$ CUP BUTTERMILK

1 LARGE EGG, BEATEN

CONFECTIONERS' SUGAR

Gently stir the strawberries and 2 tablespoons of the granulated sugar together in a bowl. Cover and refrigerate for 2 hours.

BREAK POINT
The berries can macerate for up to 4 hours.

Preheat the oven to 400°F. Butter a 10-inch cake pan.

Put the flour, baking powder, salt, and 2 tablespoons of the granulated sugar in the bowl of a food processor fitted with the steel blade. Cut in the butter until the mixture resembles fine crumbs. Add the 1 cup cream and the buttermilk and pulse to incorporate them into the dough.

Roll out the dough on a floured surface to a thickness of about 1 ½ inches.

With a 2 ½- or 3-inch round cutter, cut the biscuits into circles. Put the circles in the pan, sides touching, so the biscuits will form a "biscuit cake" when they rise. Brush the tops of the biscuits with the beaten egg and sprinkle with the remaining 1 tablespoon granulated sugar.

Bake the biscuits until they rise and turn a light golden brown, 15 to 18 minutes. Carefully remove the cake from the pan by inverting it onto a large plate, then inverting it again onto another plate, taking care to avoid breaking apart the individual biscuits. Let cool to room temperature.

(CONTINUED)

Using a long, sharp, serrated knife, slice the biscuit cake in half horizontally, and gently slide a rimless baking sheet in between the halves to lift the top from the bottom. Place the bottom on a serving plate and fill with the whipped cream and macerated strawberries. Gently replace the top of the cake and sprinkle with confectioners' sugar. Use the biscuits as a guide when cutting individual portions.

KEY LIME
CHEESECAKE PARFAIT

MAKES 10

The trademark tart and creamy aspects of a Key lime pie take a new form here, presented in a layered cheesecake parfait. Not only is this an arrestingly original presentation but it's a quicker, easier way to assemble this modernized version.

24 OUNCES (THREE 8-OUNCE PACKAGES) CREAM CHEESE

3/4 CUP PLUS 2 TABLESPOONS SUGAR

2 LARGE EGGS

2 TABLESPOONS FINELY GRATED LIME ZEST, PREFERABLY KEY LIMES, PLUS 1/3 CUP KEY LIME JUICE

2 TABLESPOONS MYERS'S RUM

1/2 CUP LIME SECTIONS, PREFERABLY KEY LIME (FROM ABOUT 3 LIMES)

1 1/2 TABLESPOONS JULIENNED FRESH MINT LEAVES

1/2 CUP CRÈME FRAÎCHE, WHIPPED UNTIL STIFF PEAKS FORM

10 SUGARED GRAHAM CRACKERS SNAPPED IN HALF

Preheat the oven to 350°F.

Put the cream cheese in a standing mixer and start the motor running. Gradually add the 3/4 cup sugar and the eggs, then the lime zest and juice. Pour this mixture into a 2-quart baking dish and set the dish in a roasting pan. Fill the pan halfway up the sides of the baking dish with hot water to create a water bath. Bake until the mixture rises slightly and firms up throughout, 40 to 45 minutes. Remove the pan from the oven and let cool and set. Remove the dish from the roasting pan, loosely cover with plastic, and refrigerate for 6 to 8 hours.

Put the rum in a small saucepan. Heat briefly, then flame with a match. When the alcohol is burned off, the rum will have reduced to about a tablespoon. Let the rum cool.

Add the lime sections, remaining 2 tablespoons sugar, and mint to the rum and stir together.

Use a pastry bag or spoon to fill 10 individual glasses three-quarters full with the chilled cheesecake mixture. Spoon about a tablespoon of the whipped crème fraîche over each serving and top with sauce. Place 2 halves of 1 graham cracker in the cheesecake and serve.

PASSION FRUIT
TOASTED COCONUT TART

MAKES ONE 10-INCH TART

After a large meal, the light, bright, acidic flavor of passion fruit is a welcome and refreshing palate cleanser. This exotic fruit tart brings that flavor, plus the very complementary crunch of toasted coconut, to a familiar format.

¾ CUP DRIED COCONUT FLAKES

6 TO 7 PASSION FRUITS

1 CUP HEAVY CREAM PLUS 1 CUP WHIPPED UNTIL FIRM

½ CUP CRÈME FRAÎCHE

8 LARGE EGG YOLKS PLUS 2 LARGE YOLKS

1 CUP GRANULATED SUGAR

1½ CUPS ALL-PURPOSE FLOUR

1 CUP CONFECTIONERS' SUGAR

¼ TEASPOON FINE SALT

¼ CUP MILK

3 TABLESPOONS COLD UNSALTED BUTTER, FINELY DICED, PLUS MORE FOR GREASING THE TIN

Preheat the oven to 325°F.

Spread out the coconut on a baking sheet and bake until lightly toasted, approximately 5 minutes, shaking the pan to ensure even cooking. Set aside.

To make the passion fruit custard, cut the passion fruits in half and place the pulp in a mesh strainer. Press the pulp through the strainer into a bowl, until you have 1½ cups of pulp and juice. Discard the seeds that remain in the strainer. Beat the unwhipped cream, crème fraîche, 8 yolks, and granulated sugar into the puree and chill until cold.

BREAK POINT
The custard can be covered and refrigerated overnight. When ready to proceed, preheat the oven to 325°F.

To make the pastry crust, put the flour, confectioners' sugar, and salt in a food processor and pulse to combine. Add the milk, butter, and remaining 2 yolks in batches, pulsing until the dough begins to clump. When the dough has come together, transfer it to a well-floured surface.

Roll the dough out to a thickness of about ¼ inch and a diameter just larger than a 10-inch tart tin. Butter the tin and put the dough in it, pressing it against the sides. Cover with aluminum foil and fill it with dried beans or rice. Bake until light golden brown, approximately 25 minutes.

Lower the oven temperature to 325°F. Remove the foil and beans and pour the custard into the shell. Return to the oven and bake until the custard firms up, 30 to 35 minutes. Let the tart cool.

(CONTINUED)

When the tart is cool, cover and refrigerate until cold, at least 4 hours.

When ready to serve, evenly coat the surface of the tart with the whipped cream. Sprinkle with the coconut and slice into 10 servings.

VANILLA
CRÈME BRÛLÉE

SERVES 6

The richness of custard-based desserts (ice cream, flan, crème brûlée, etc.) is determined by the number of egg yolks. This crème brûlée attains maximum, steakhouse-appropriate intensity with one large yolk per serving. The recipe uses a home-cook–friendly method of browning the sugar under the broiler, but you can now purchase small propane torches designed expressly for this purpose. If you happen to own one, it's a fun, restaurant-style alternative to finish these off.

1½ CUPS HEAVY CREAM

I VANILLA BEAN, SPLIT AND SCRAPED

¾ CUP SUGAR

6 EXTRA-LARGE EGG YOLKS

Preheat the oven to 325°F.

Put the cream, vanilla bean, and ½ cup of the sugar in a saucepan and bring to a boil over medium heat. Immediately remove the pot from the heat and set it aside.

Put the yolks in a bowl and whisk well. Add a small amount of the hot cream to the egg yolks, whisking to temper the yolks, then whisk the yolks into the cream in the pot and continue whisking for 1 minute. Use tongs or a slotted spoon to remove and discard the vanilla bean.

Divide the custard among 6 shallow 6-ounce ramekins. Put the ramekins in a roasting pan and fill the pan halfway up the sides of the ramekins with warm water.

Put the pan in the oven and bake until the custards are firm, 40 to 45 minutes.

Remove the pan from the oven, carefully remove the ramekins from the pan, let cool to room temperature, then loosely cover with plastic wrap and refrigerate for 4 hours.

BREAK POINT
The cooked custards can be refrigerated overnight.

Preheat the broiler.

Evenly sprinkle the remaining ¼ cup sugar over the chilled crème brûlées. Broil until the sugar is caramelized to a golden brown, 2 to 3 minutes, depending on the broiler temperature. Serve immediately while the sugar is still warm.

BONUS POINTS

COFFEE CRÈME BRÛLÉE

Replace the vanilla bean with 1 tablespoon coffee granules and 3 tablespoons Kahlúa.

CHOCOLATE CRÈME BRÛLÉE

Omit the vanilla bean and increase the cream to 2 cups. Begin by melting 6 ounces semisweet chocolate in a double boiler, then proceed with the recipe. Whisk the melted chocolate into the yolk-cream mixture just before pouring into the ramekins.

CHOCOLATE CAKE

A scaled-down version of our classic Strip House twenty-four-layer chocolate cake, this is a chocolate-lover's fantasy come to life with layers of chocolate cake sandwiching chocolate custard.

CUSTARD

1¾ CUPS MILK

1½ CUPS HEAVY CREAM

2 LARGE EGGS PLUS 3 LARGE EGG YOLKS

¾ CUP SUGAR

1 TEASPOON FINE SALT

3 TABLESPOONS CORNSTARCH

¾ CUP ALL-PURPOSE FLOUR

4 OUNCES SEMISWEET CHOCOLATE, ROUGHLY CHOPPED

1 TABLESPOON VANILLA EXTRACT

Scald the milk and cream in a saucepan. Remove the pan from the heat and set aside.

Whisk the eggs and yolks together in a bowl. Gradually add the sugar, beating until the mixture is thick and light in color. Whisk in the salt, cornstarch, and flour.

Temper the egg mixture by adding about a third of the hot milk to the eggs, then pour the egg mixture back into the saucepan. Stir continuously over low heat until the mixture comes to a boil and thickens. At the boiling point, whisk until smooth. Be sure to reach into the bend of the saucepan to incorporate thoroughly. Let the custard simmer for about 1 minute.

Remove the pan from the heat and stir in the chocolate. Let stand until the chocolate melts, 2 to 3 minutes. Stir in the vanilla.

Pour the mixture into a bowl and refrigerate until firm, at least 2 to 3 hours.

BREAK POINT
The custard can be made up to 2 days ahead of time.

CHOCOLATE CAKE

2 CUPS CAKE FLOUR

1½ TEASPOONS BAKING SODA

½ TEASPOON BAKING POWDER

1½ TEASPOONS FINE SALT

⅔ CUP BEST-QUALITY COCOA POWDER

½ POUND (2 STICKS) UNSALTED BUTTER, SOFTENED AT ROOM TEMPERATURE, PLUS MORE FOR GREASING THE PAN

2 CUPS SUGAR, PLUS MORE FOR SUGARING THE PAN

6 LARGE EGGS

1 CUP MILK

1 CUP BREWED COFFEE, PLUS MORE IF NEEDED

Preheat the oven to 350°F.

Sift the flour, baking soda, baking powder, salt, and cocoa powder 3 times into a bowl.

Using an electric mixer, cream the softened butter and sugar together in a mixing bowl until all of the sugar is incorporated. Slowly add the eggs and mix until light and creamy. Add half of the sifted dry ingredients and fold them into the creamy mixture. Add ½ cup of the milk and ½ cup of the coffee. Repeat with the remaining dry ingredients, milk, and coffee.

Butter and sugar a 9-inch loaf pan. Pour the cake batter evenly into the pan. (It should come about ½ inch from the top of the pan. Depending on the shape of your pan, you might have some batter left over, which you can discard. Or bake the leftover cake in a warm oven, make crumbs with it, and use it to top ice cream.) Set the pan on a baking sheet to catch any spills and bake until the cake is set and a toothpick inserted in the center comes out clean, 45 to 50 minutes.

Remove the pan from the oven and let cool for 1 hour at room temperature. Carefully turn the cake out onto a wire rack and let it finish cooling there.

Cut the top ½ inch off the cake and place it on a baking sheet. Return it to the oven, which should still be slightly warm from baking. Let the cake top dry out for about 1 hour in the oven, then pulse into crumbs using a food processor. Set aside.

Cut 1 layer, 1 inch thick, for the bottom of the cake, then slice the remaining sponge cake into four 1-inch layers.

Spread each layer with a thin layer of chocolate custard. Stack the layers, cover with plastic wrap, and refrigerate for 2 to 12 hours.

Thin the remaining custard with just enough coffee to make it spreadable. Lightly ice the exterior of the cake with this mixture and press the cake crumbs onto the sides of the cake.

Transfer to a serving plate and slice into 1½-inch slices to serve.

CREAMY MASCARPONE CHEESECAKE
WITH **MARINATED FRESH RASPBERRIES**

MAKES ONE 9-INCH CAKE

One of the most popular desserts at Strip House is our cheesecake, served in enormous slabs that are usually shared by two to four people from the center of the table. It's everything that a cheesecake should be, rich, creamy, and deeply satisfying. Here, it's paired with marinated berries that cut and complement its flavor and texture.

2 POUNDS (FOUR 8-OUNCE PACKAGES) CREAM CHEESE

6 OUNCES ($\frac{3}{4}$ CUP) MASCARPONE CHEESE

$1\frac{1}{4}$ CUPS PLUS 1 TABLESPOON SUGAR

1 TABLESPOON VANILLA EXTRACT

6 LARGE EGGS

$1\frac{1}{4}$ CUPS GRAHAM CRACKER CRUMBS (FROM ABOUT 10 WHOLE GRAHAM CRACKERS)

4 TABLESPOONS ($\frac{1}{2}$ STICK) UNSALTED BUTTER, MELTED

$\frac{1}{2}$ TEASPOON GROUND CINNAMON

1 PINT FRESH RASPBERRIES

2 TEASPOONS FINELY GRATED LEMON ZEST PLUS $1\frac{1}{2}$ TEASPOONS FRESHLY SQUEEZED LEMON JUICE

$\frac{1}{4}$ CUP ORANGE JUICE

3 FRESH MINT SPRIGS, THINLY SLICED

To make the batter, put the cream cheese, mascarpone, $1\frac{1}{4}$ cups sugar, and vanilla extract in the bowl of a mixer fitted with the paddle attachment and paddle until the ingredients are well incorporated and smooth. Slowly add the eggs until well incorporated. Strain the mixture through a sieve set over a bowl.

BREAK POINT
The batter can be covered and refrigerated for up to 2 days.

Preheat the oven to 325°F.

Wrap the bottom of a 9-inch springform pan with aluminum foil. Mix the graham crackers, butter, and cinnamon to a paste in a bowl. Pour into the pan, pressing the mixture down evenly.

Pour in the cheesecake batter. Place the pan in an ovenproof dish and fill halfway up the sides of the pan with cold water.

Bake for 2 hours. Remove from the oven and let cool to room temperature. Refrigerate overnight before serving.

At least 2 hours before serving, put the raspberries, lemon zest and juice, orange juice, remaining 1 tablespoon sugar, and mint in a bowl and stir together gently. Cover and refrigerate for 2 hours.

BREAK POINT
The berries can be refrigerated for up to 4 hours.

To serve, slice the cheesecake into individual servings. Put each slice in the center of a dessert plate and spoon 2 tablespoons of the berries around the perimeter of each plate.

DRESS-UPS
FOR STORE-BOUGHT ICE CREAM

ALL RECIPES SERVE 8 TO 10

We all have a limited amount of time to spend in the kitchen. And while there's nothing like homemade ice cream, I think it's a much better idea to budget your time by purchasing a high-quality supermarket brand and making your own toppings. Any or all of these toppings have the power to turn any ice cream into something special.

MACERATED BERRIES

I TEASPOON FINELY GRATED LEMON ZEST PLUS 2 TEASPOONS FRESHLY SQUEEZED LEMON JUICE

I TEASPOON JULIENNED FRESH MINT LEAVES

I TEASPOON FINELY GRATED ORANGE ZEST

2 TABLESPOONS FRESHLY SQUEEZED ORANGE JUICE

I CUP BLACKBERRIES

I CUP RASPBERRIES

I CUP BLUEBERRIES

1½ CUPS STRAWBERRIES, STEMMED AND QUARTERED

Stir the lemon zest and juice, mint, and orange zest and juice together in a bowl. Put the blackberries, raspberries, blueberries, and strawberries in another bowl and pour the mixture over the berries. Let macerate for 30 minutes before serving.

The berries can be covered and refrigerated for up to 4 hours.

GRILLED FRUIT

2 POUNDS SUMMER FRUIT, SUCH AS RIPE NECTARINES, PEACHES, PLUMS, LARGE STRAWBERRIES, EVEN BANANAS AND UNPEELED APPLES, CUT INTO WEDGES

On an outdoor grill

On a well-cleaned and seasoned grill over high heat, grill the fruit wedges cut side down, until softened and the wedges have apparent grill marks. (Timing will vary greatly, depending on the type of fruit and the ripeness.) Turn to grill on the skin side, then move the fruit onto aluminum foil over indirect heat, close the grill, and continue to cook, monitoring closely, until the fruit softens and starts to melt down onto its skin and the sugars have caramelized. Don't grill too long; the grill time is determined by the ripeness of the fruit and the heat of the grill. Dice the grilled fruit.

(CONTINUED)

In a cast-iron pan

Heat a cast-iron grill pan over high heat. Season the grill pan with a light coating of corn oil, canola oil, or grapeseed oil and cook the fruit wedges until softened and the sugars are caramelized, 2 to 3 minutes.

BOURBON SAUCE

2 CUPS SUGAR

2 TABLESPOONS BOURBON, SUCH AS JIM BEAM OR JACK DANIEL'S

½ CUP HEAVY CREAM

Put the sugar and ½ cup water in a heavy-bottomed, 4- or 5-quart, stainless-steel saucepan and heat over medium-high heat, stirring with a fork or wooden spoon until all the sugar is dissolved, approximately 5 minutes. Continue cooking, carefully swirling the pan, until the syrup begins to turn brown.

When the sugar becomes darker, remove the pan from the stove and pour in the bourbon and cream. (Be careful: the sugar will start to boil.) Stir until well incorporated, then let cool to room temperature before serving.

The sauce can be covered and refrigerated for up to 3 days.

MACADAMIA NUT CRUNCH

I CUP SUGAR

1¼ CUPS UNSALTED CRACKED MACADAMIA NUTS (FROM 5 TO 6 OUNCES NUTS)

Line a baking pan with parchment paper and set it aside.

Put the sugar and ½ cup water in a heavy-bottomed, stainless-steel pot. Set over medium-high heat and cook, stirring with a fork or wooden spoon, until all the sugar is dissolved, approximately 3 minutes. Continue to simmer until the mixture begins to turn a light-golden color, carefully swirling the pan to keep it from sticking or scorching.

Add the macadamia nuts and stir well to coat all of the nuts with the caramel. Carefully pour the nuts in a single layer over the parchment-paper-lined baking sheet. Let cool and harden at room temperature.

The crunch can be covered and kept for up to 2 days in a dry place.

MAPLE-WALNUT SAUCE

1½ CUPS CRACKED WALNUTS
(FROM 6 OUNCES NUTS)

1¼ CUPS MAPLE SYRUP

½ CUP MOLASSES

½ TEASPOON VANILLA EXTRACT

2 TEASPOONS FINELY GRATED
ORANGE ZEST

¾ CUP FRESHLY SQUEEZED
ORANGE JUICE

2 TABLESPOONS GRAND MARNIER,
OPTIONAL

Toast the walnuts in a sauté pan over medium heat until fragrant, approximately 4 minutes. Transfer to a bowl and set aside to cool.

Heat the syrup, molasses, vanilla, orange zest, orange juice, and Grand Marnier, if using, in a small, heavy-bottomed saucepan over medium heat. Add the walnuts and stir to coat with the syrup. Cook, stirring, over medium-low heat until thickened, 10 to 12 minutes. Transfer to a small bowl and let cool to room temperature.

The walnuts can be covered and refrigerated for up to 2 days. Let come to room temperature before serving.

CHOCOLATE-PECAN BROWNIES

6 OUNCES (1½ STICKS) UNSALTED
BUTTER, PLUS MORE FOR GREASING
THE PAN

¾ CUP COCOA POWDER

1 CUP SUGAR

¾ TEASPOON VANILLA EXTRACT

2 LARGE EGGS

½ CUP ALL-PURPOSE FLOUR

½ CUP CRACKED PECANS
(FROM 2 OUNCES NUTS)

Preheat the oven to 325°F. Lightly butter an 8-inch square baking pan.

Melt the butter in a saucepan. Put the cocoa powder and sugar in a large bowl, add the butter, and stir until everything is evenly combined. Stir in the vanilla and then beat in 1 egg at a time with an electric beater. Add the flour, stirring until incorporated. Add the nuts and stir to combine.

Transfer to the baking pan and bake for 20 minutes, until just set. Let cook, then cut into 8 to 10 brownies.

TO DRINK

Selecting a wine to go with a meal or a particular dish is ultimately a matter of personal taste. But it never hurts to have the input of a professional sommelier in making those decisions. Having the right wine paired with a meal can really take the senses on a ride. With all that in mind, this chart offers you guidance in selecting wines to go with the dishes in this book.

The categories correspond to those in the "To Drink" listing at the end of the recipes. "Cheap and Clever" ($16 or less) are everyday wines that may surprise you with their quality; "Above Average" ($16 to $35) are small splurges that will pay big dividends in taste and complexity; and "Cellar Selections" ($35 and over) are wines that cost a lot, but in my opinion are worth every cent.

Where no vintage (year) is listed, that's because many producers are able to create the same flavor characteristics year in and year out. Where a vintage is indicated, it refers to an especially successful bottling that's worth seeking out.

These wines should all be relatively easy to come by, either in your local wine store or from an online source. My hope is that you'll have no trouble procuring at least one of the wines in each price range of each category.

WINES

WHITE	CHEAP AND CLEVER UP TO $16	ABOVE AVERAGE $16–$35	CELLAR SELECTIONS $35 AND OVER
Aromatic	Freemark Abbey Viognier, USA	Clos St. Landelin Gewürztraminer, Alsace	Henschke Gewürztraminer, Australia
	Trimbach Riesling, Alsace	Bonterra Viognier, USA	Mt. Harlen Calera Viognier, USA
	Lingenfelder Riesling, Germany	Fairview Viognier, South Africa	Joh. Jos Prum Weh. Son. Auslese, Germany
Oaky/Full-Bodied	Ravenswood Chardonnay, USA	Matanzas Creek Chardonnay, USA	Talbott Sleepy Hollow Chardonnay, USA
	Yalumba Chardonnay, Australia	Chateau Montelena Chardonnay, USA	Kistler Chardonnay, USA
	Domaine Anne Gros Bourgogne Blanc, France	Henschke Chardonnay, Australia	Far Niente Chardonnay, USA
Crisp/Fresh	Casa Lapostolle Sauvignon Blanc, Chile	Chalk Hill Sauvignon Blanc, USA	J. Moreau, Chablis Grand Cru, Burgundy, France
	Kenwood Sauvignon Blanc, USA	JJ Vincent, Pouilly-Fuisse, Burgundy, France	Voss Winery Sauvignon Blanc, USA
	Etienne Sauzet 2001 White Burgundy, France	Pascal Jolivet Sancerre Blanc, France	Livio Felluga Pinot Grigio, Italy
Light/Floral	Zenato Pinot Grigio, Italy	Forefathers Sauvignon Blanc, New Zealand	Failla Viognier, USA
	Bonny Doon Pacific Rim Riesling, USA	Castle Vineyards Viognier, USA	Domaine Louis Latour Corton-Charlemagne, Grand Cru, France
	Rosemount Traminer-Riesling, Australia	Cape Mentelle Semillon/ Sauvignon, Australia	Merryvale Starmont Sauvignon Blanc, USA
RED			
Full-Bodied/ Tannic	Mondavi-Woodbridge Cabernet Sauvignon, USA	Grgich Hills Cabernet Sauvignon, USA	Silver Oak Cabernet Sauvignon, USA
	Cousino Macul Cabernet Sauvignon, Chile	Château de Lescours St. Emilion, France	Kenwood Artist Series Cabernet Sauvignon, USA
	Clos du Bois Cabernet Sauvignon, USA	Pirramimma Shiraz 2001, Australia	Marchesi di Barolo Cannubi, Italy
			Château Pichon-Lalande, Pauillac, France
Light/Fruit-Forward	Glass Mountain Merlot, USA	Saintsbury Pinot Noir, USA	Ponzi Reserve Pinot Noir, USA
	Castle Rock Pinot Noir, USA	Batasiolo Barbera D'Alba Sovrana, Italy	Beaune Clos des Mouches 1er Cru 1999, France
	Georges Duboeuf Beaujolais Villages, France	Castello di Volpaia Chianti Classico Riserva, Italy	Peregrine Pinot Noir, New Zealand
	Sierra Cantabria Rioja, Spain	Coto de Imaz Grand Reserve Rioja, Spain	

	CHEAP AND CLEVER UP TO $16	ABOVE AVERAGE $16–$35	CELLAR SELECTIONS $35 AND OVER
Smooth/Medium-Bodied	Rosemount Shiraz, Australia	Louis Jadot Chambolle-Musigny Les Fuées Red Burgundy, France	St. Clement Oroppas, USA
	Torres 2000 Atrium Merlot, Spain	Jordan Cabernet Sauvignon, USA	Shafer Merlot, USA
	Cosentino Cabernet Franc, USA	Chateau Ste. Michelle Merlot, USA	Concha y Toro 2000 Don Melchor Private Reserve Cabernet Sauvignon, Chile
	Castello di Monastero Chianti Classico, Italy		
Spicy	Gloria's "Old Vines" Zinfandel, USA	Ridge Geyersville Zinfandel, USA	Louis Jadot Clos Saint-Denis Red Burgundy, France
	Qupé Syrah, USA	Penfolds Bin 28 Kalimna Shiraz 2000, South Australia	Marques de Riscal Baron de Chirel Reserva Rioja, Spain
	Chameleon Cellars 2000 Sangiovese, USA	Jaboulet Côte Rôtie Les Jumelles, France	Biale Zinfandel, USA
		Joel Gott Zinfandel, USA	M. Chapoutier Côte Rôtie, France

OTHER

	CHEAP AND CLEVER UP TO $16	ABOVE AVERAGE $16–$35	CELLAR SELECTIONS $35 AND OVER
Fizzy/Sparkling	Gruet, USA	Pommery Brut NV, France	Krug Grande Cuvee, France
	Roederer Estate, USA	Veuve Clicquot Yellow Label Brut NV, France	Schramsberg J. Schram Tete de Cuvee, USA
	Bouvet Brut, France	Moët & Chandon Rosé NV, France	Moët & Chandon Dom Perignon, France
	Mionetto Il Prosecco Spumante, Italy		
Rosé	Beringer White Zinfandel, USA	Domaine Ott Rosé, France	Jaboulet Tavel, France
	Sanford Pinot Noir Vin Gris, USA	Bonny Doon Vin Gris de Cigare, USA	Turkey Flat Rosé, Australia
Sweet	Lakeview Cellars Vidal Icewine, Canada	Peter Jacob Kuhn Oestricher Lenchen Spatlese Riesling, Germany	Château d'Yquem Sauternes, France
	Pervini Primo Amore Primitivo, Italy	Bonny Doon Muscat Vin de Glaciere, USA	Oremus Tokaji, Hungary

BEERS

Beer can sometimes be just as good a choice as wine to go with a meal. It may never match wine for sheer variety and complexity, but there are a number of beers that have their time and place at the table. In order to match up with the dishes in the book, this chart is based on flavor profile and "weight" rather than on brewing style.

LIGHT-BODIED

Amstel Light
Anchor Steam
Beck's
Jever Pilsner
Pilsner Urquell
Rouge Mogul Ale

BLOND

Brooklyn East India Pale Ale
Celis White
Hefe Weizen

AMBER

Bass Ale
Samuel Smith Nut Brown Ale
San Miguel Dark Lager
Sierra Nevada Pale Ale
Stoudt's Pale Ale

RICH/DARK

Brooklyn Black Chocolate Stout
Catamount Porter
Samuel Smith Oatmeal Stout
Spaten Munich Optimator

MEAT BY MAIL

In my experience, these are the best mail-order companies from which to order.

ALLEN BROTHERS
Chicago, Illinois
800–957–0111
www.allenbrothers.com
This company sells a full range of poultry and meats, from duck to pork to veal.

THE GLAZIER GROUP
www.theglaziergroup.com
Of course I'm partial to my own restaurants' standards. In addition to our steaks, we sell our proprietary steak sauces, chocolate cake, and tabletop items. You can read more about our restaurants at the Web site.

LOBEL'S
New York, New York
877–783–4512
www.lobels.com
This online butcher shop, an extension of a New York City institution, is a reliable source of poultry and meats. They also make and sell their own hot dogs.

NIMAN RANCH
Oakland, California
866–808–0340
www.nimanranch.com
One of the most popular suppliers of meats to New York City chefs, this California-based company specializes in natural and antibiotic-free cuts of pork, beef, and veal and often has hard-to-find specialty cuts.

STOCKYARDS
Chicago, Illinois
877–785–9273
www.stockyards.com
From seafood to beef, you can order a variety of cuts from this restaurant purveyor.

INDEX